Letters
George Brenton Laurie

(commanding 1st Battn Royal Irish Rifles) Dated
November 4th, 1914-March 11th, 1915

George Brenton Laurie

Editor: Florence Vere-Laurie

Alpha Editions

This edition published in 2022

ISBN : 9789356783430

Design and Setting By
Alpha Editions
www.alphaedis.com
Email - info@alphaedis.com

As per information held with us this book is in Public Domain.
This book is a reproduction of an important historical work. Alpha Editions uses the best technology to reproduce historical work in the same manner it was first published to preserve its original nature. Any marks or number seen are left intentionally to preserve its true form.

Contents

TO HALIBURTON, BLANCHE, AND SYDNEY. ....- 1 -

FOREWORD ....- 3 -

SKETCH OF LIEUT.-COLONEL LAURIE'S CAREER. ....- 5 -

LETTERS OF NOVEMBER, 1914. ....- 7 -

LETTERS OF DECEMBER, 1914. ....- 23 -

"CHRISTMAS IN THE CRIMEA. ....- 41 -

LETTERS OF JANUARY, 1915. ....- 51 -

LETTERS OF FEBRUARY, 1915. ....- 70 -

LETTERS OF MARCH, 1915. ....- 93 -

"AFTERWARDS." ....- 104 -

THE LATE COLONEL LAURIE. ....- 111 -

R.I. RIFLES ENGAGED. ....- 113 -

FROM NEUVE CHAPELLE. ....- 115 -

THE ROYAL IRISH RIFLES. ....- 117 -

SPECIAL ORDER OF THE DAY BY
HIS MAJESTY THE KING.[14]..- 119 -

R.I.R.'s AT NEUVE CHAPELLE. ....- 120 -

"THE MAN OF SORROWS."..- 121 -

TO HALIBURTON, BLANCHE, AND SYDNEY.

My dear Children,

I dedicate this little volume to you in memory of your father, who, as you know, fell on March 12th, 1915, in the Battle of Neuve Chapelle. These Letters, which were written to me from France during the first winter of the World War, do not in any way pretend to literary attainment; they are just the simple letters of a soldier recording as a diary the daily doings of his regiment at the front.

Often were they penned under great difficulties, and many a time under a rain of fire. The accounts of the awful loss of life and the discomforts experienced, both by officers and men unused to such severe climatic conditions, are sometimes heart-rending, and they make the reading sad.

Touches, however, of his natural cheerfulness relieve the greyness of the situation, and at times one can almost hear the lightheartedness of a schoolboy speaking.

Your father cared for his regiment as a father cares for his child, and was beloved by it. He obtained his commission in 1885 at 18 years of age, and was, curiously enough, the last officer to enter the British Army with the rank of a full Lieutenant. Had he lived till the following September, he would have been 30 years in the Royal Irish Rifles.

A short sketch of his life and military career is given in this book, and reference is made to the pleasure he took in being chosen to write the History of his Regiment, completed in 1914. He was also devoted to all kinds of sport as a pastime; but I will not write of these things; rather would I speak of his great wish to win fresh laurels for his regiment, and of how proud he was when, after the long, dreary winter in the trenches, the Royal Irish Rifles were the first to enter the village of Neuve Chapelle. But above all would I counsel you to follow his example in his faithful attention to duty, fulfilling the French proverb, "Faites ce que doit advienne que pourra."

He died as a true soldier, leading his men, and what better death could be desired? He now lies in the British military cemetery of Pont du Hem, midway between Neuve Chapelle and Estaires, not far from Bethune in Northern France, and a little wooden cross marks the spot.

F. VERE-LAURIE.

CARLTON HALL,
CARLTON-ON-TRENT, NOTTS.
May 12th, 1921.

FOREWORD

By Lieut.-Colonel Sir John Ross of Bladensburg, K.C.B., K.C.V.O. *(late Coldstream Guards).*

Colonel George Laurie came from a military family. His father a distinguished General, and his uncle both served in the Crimea and elsewhere, and many of his near relations joined the army, and were well-known zealous soldiers of their Sovereign. His elder brother fell in the Boer War in the beginning of this century, and he himself saw active service in the Sudan and in South Africa, before he landed in France to take his share in the great World War. On being promoted to the command of his battalion, he joined it at Kamptee in India, and this obliged him to leave his wife and family at home, for young children are not able to live in that tropical, very hot and unhealthy district. From that station, with scarcely any opportunity of seeing them again, he was launched into the severities of a cold and wet winter in a water-logged part of Flanders. His experiences are graphically told in his letters, and they will show how much our gallant troops had to endure when engaged in the terrible conflict which the ambition of Prussia had provoked, and with what fortitude and courage they defended the country from the serious dangers that then menaced it.

All who have read these interesting letters will, I think, perceive that one dominant feature in Colonel Laurie's character was a keen and all-pervading sense of duty, and an earnest determination to discharge it in every circumstance as thoroughly and as completely as possible. Never did he spare himself. What he had to exact from others, that he sternly imposed upon himself; and he fully shared with his men all the dangers and all the hardships of the war, with serene good temper and with a cheerful spirit. This fine disposition, which he himself had trained by self-discipline, ensured the prompt and willing obedience of his subordinates, and endeared him to all who were committed to his charge; it also secured for him the respect and the confidence of his superiors, who were well aware that every order they gave him would be carried out to the letter with prudence and with strict fidelity.

As he had married a beloved niece, I had many opportunities of observing his character, and I did not fail to recognize how devoted he was to his regiment and to the military career he had embraced and how thoroughly he was imbued with this great sense of duty. He had, moreover, considerable literary ability, and wrote a very excellent History of the Royal

Irish Rifles; he also translated from the French an interesting account of the conquest of Algiers. In short, he took pains to learn the many details of his noble profession, and to make himself an efficient officer. Had he survived, my belief is that he would have advanced far as a soldier; for he combined with a studious earnest mind, much activity of body, and a sincere love for outdoor sport and manly exercise.

His letters show his affectionate nature; his care for his family and for his officers and men; and his solicitude for all with whom he was brought in contact. His sympathies were quick and real; and he felt the responsibilities of his position, and what he owed to those who belonged to him, or who were placed under his command. And last, but by no means least, there are many short expressions in the letters to show the deep and all-absorbing feeling he entertained for Religion, and how his whole life was guided by the Faith that was in him. May his memory prove to be an incentive to his young family, so early and so cruelly deprived of the care of a loving father, to imitate his sterling qualities of head and heart!

SKETCH OF LIEUT.-COLONEL LAURIE'S CAREER.

(From the "Bond of Sacrifice," reproduced by permission of the Editor.)

George Brenton Laurie was born at Halifax, Nova Scotia, on October 13th, 1867. He was the eldest surviving son of the late Lieut.-General John Wimburn Laurie, C.B., M.P., of 47, Porchester Terrace, London, and of Mrs. Laurie, of Oakfield, Nova Scotia.

He was grandson of the Hon. Enos Collins, M.L.C., of Gorse Brook, Halifax, and great-grandson of Sir Brenton Haliburton, Chief Justice of Nova Scotia. He was educated at Galt Collegiate Institute, Ontario, and at the Picton Academy, from whence he passed into the Royal Military College, Kingston, Canada, in 1883. He joined the Royal Irish Rifles as a Lieutenant in September, 1885, going with them to Gibraltar in 1886, and on to Egypt in 1888. He took part in the Nile Campaign in 1889, but, contracting smallpox at Assouan, he was sent home to recover, and spent two years at the Depot at Belfast, rejoining his battalion in Malta. He was promoted Captain in 1893, and when the Rifles came back to home service he obtained an Adjutancy of Volunteers in Devonshire in October, 1896, and from that date until March, 1901, by ceaseless energy he brought the battalion to full strength and high efficiency.

In March, 1901, he was appointed a special service officer, including the command of a mounted infantry battalion for the South African War. He was present at operations in the Transvaal, Orange River Colony, and Cape Colony, between April, 1901, and May, 1902, having been Mentioned in Despatches for his services (London Gazette, July 29th, 1902), also receiving the Queen's Medal with five clasps.

After peace was signed he served in Ireland, and in October, 1904, obtained his majority. Afterwards he served in England till, becoming Lieut.-Colonel in 1912, he went out to India to take command of the 1st Battalion Royal Irish Rifles. He was deeply engaged at this time in writing the History of his Regiment, a work soon officially accepted and highly praised. He had previously written a history of "The French in Morocco," compiled from many sources during his years in the Mediterranean.

When the European War broke out in August, 1914, he was at Aden with his battalion, and until anxiety in Somaliland was allayed the Irish

Rifles were detained there, only reaching France in November. They spent the winter in the trenches, taking their share in the fierce fighting in December.

On March 10th, 1915, they took part in the attack on Neuve Chapelle, and were the first battalion to reach the village, but losses were heavy. A sergeant-major wrote: "Our Colonel was everywhere, encouraging his men, and seeming to bear a charmed life. He knew no fear, and walked quietly in front of us as if no bombardment were going on."

On Friday evening, March 12th, a fresh assault was ordered. Lieut.-Colonel Laurie rallied his exhausted men, and, calling out "Follow me! I will lead you!" he sprang over the parapet, revolver in hand. A moment later he fell shot through the head. He was buried with his fallen officers and men in a garden near Neuve Chapelle.

During this war he was twice Mentioned in Despatches (*Gazette*, January 14th, 1915; and after his death, May 31st, 1915).

Lieut.-Colonel Laurie, who was a member of the Army and Navy and the United Service Clubs, was fond of hunting, and went out regularly with the Devon and Somerset hounds. He also hunted in Ireland, and in Nottinghamshire with the Rufford, and played polo.

He married, in September, 1905, Florence Clementina Vere Skeffington, eldest daughter of the late Hon. Sydney William Skeffington, and left three children—George Haliburton, born August, 1906; Blanche, born 1907; and Sydney Vere, born 1910.

LETTERS OF NOVEMBER, 1914.

Telegram, November 4th, 1914:

"Get gun oiled."

[*Note.*—This was a private code message sent to me in London signifying that the 1st Battalion Royal Irish Rifles was ordered to France with the 25th Brigade, 8th Division, on November 5th, 1914. Information of the day of departure was not permitted beforehand.—F.V.L.]

HURSTLEY PARK CAMP,
Winchester.
November 5th, 1914.

My dear F——.

I telegraphed to you yesterday not to worry about any more equipment for me, as I should not be able to get the things, no matter how soon you sent them. We have had our arrangements put back twelve hours, but even that makes no difference; I shall rub along somehow.

The Camp is up to our necks in mud. Fortunately, the weather is mild, though we shall have it cold enough later on. Any warm clothes, etc., for the Battalion are being sent to you to be distributed to us in a short time. Then the men will appreciate them more. I should forward them only as you get the funds.

Capt. Cinnamond is still in bed with lumbago, whilst Major Weir is staying behind too. Capt. Allgood comes with me. I cannot give you any more news, as it might let things out. I had a lot to do yesterday, and dropped to sleep after dinner sitting in a high chair about 8.45 p.m.!

Yours, etc....
G——.

Postcard from—
Southampton,
November 5th, 1914.

We had a wet march to this place, and are now on a transport which ought to land us in France to-morrow. So far everything has gone most prosperously with us. Curious that the day you left Winchester I should have got the order to move! I believe the sea is fairly smooth; am getting the last few horses and wagons aboard. Heard to-day that the Remount have bought my chestnut horse "Goldfinch."

G.B.L.

FRANCE,
ON ACTIVE SERVICE, B.E.F.
November 7th, 1914.

My dear F——.

We had a very smooth run across to ... and then lay out for about 20 hours. Fortunately, it still remained perfectly calm, and we got in at 2 a.m., having only a slight collision with another steamer. We left the ship this morning and went into a rest camp to get ourselves thoroughly fitted out. We were told that "French" wanted us badly, as he expected to have the Germans back on the Rhine shortly, which may or may not be! Anyhow, our "rest" will not last many hours! There is a thick fog at present, so I cannot tell you what the whole place is like; but the lanes as we came along reminded me of England, say Ore near Hastings. I saw that your cousin Herbert Stepney was killed,[1] and his mother will be wild about him....

A Naval Embarkation Officer came up to me at our embarking post—Southampton—and asked where Laurie was! I told him, remarking: "I know your face!" He was Captain Perfect from Rostrevor. He said that poor Major Nugent of Bally Edmond died rather suddenly two days ago. Perfect then introduced me to the Captain of the ship, who rejoiced in the name of "Spratt," with the result that I was given half his cabin coming over. We had to feed ourselves, or, rather, we bought some cooked food by arrangement. Here we have secured bread and butter and condensed milk, and we are now waiting for our transport to come up from the harbour to get some warm tea.

I will let you know as much as I can as we go along. Of course it is impossible to tell you where we are, etc.... If you want to know about German atrocities, read *Nash's Magazine* for November. I just saw it.

Yours....
G——.

On Active Service.
November 8th, 1914.

That was as far as I got in my descriptions to you when I had to rush off with my transport wagon and Quartermaster to complete the equipment which had not been given us in England. This lasted until 11.30 p.m. in a strange country with thick fog, five miles to go, and none of us able to speak French! However, I came home about 7 o'clock in the morning to fix other urgent matters up. The night was not so very cold.

Being an early bird, I varied matters this morning by calling my officers! Major Baker[2] is splendid.

After Church parade, reading the service myself, I have been generally hustling things, and am going out for a route march at 2 p.m. to-day. The sun is finally dispersing the fog, so we shall get an opportunity of drilling together. We have practically never done so yet; and I am really appalled at what might be the consequences of going into action with the men unpractised. Few of them have been on active service before, and it will all have to be taught under fire.... Since I have managed to get a pair of boots for myself from the Ordnance, I now go dry-footed for a change! I shall probably send you home my good uniform ones to keep for me, as they were made rather too tight for this sort of work. If I live through it, I will be able to wear them all out. If not, it will not matter much to me....

I expect you are having your shoot to-morrow and next day, and I hope it will be a success.

Yours....
G——.

November 9th, 1914.

I may not have time to write to you again for some days, so first, please accept my thanks for the waterproof sheet, and all the other things you bought. Unfortunately I shall not be able to carry them with me, so the lot must be returned to the Army and Navy Stores....

I think I told you that "Goldfinch," my chestnut horse, has been sold to the Government, and the roan "Khaki" I sent to Mrs. Clinton-Baker at Bayfordbury. One of my new horses rolled over me yesterday, but beyond bending my sword and tearing one of my leggings did me no damage, though Major Baker thought at first that my leg was broken! It is colder to-day. We were astonished to see a number of French soldiers about; one imagined they would be up at the Front fighting. Also there seemed to be a lot of young men who might have been out doing a little for their country.

Many of the women are in mourning here. My servant told me that most of our men had now got gloves, and that it was surprising the care they took of them, as they were generally not so careful; but they knew that they would want them; so I am very glad that you have got extra ones, for they do not last long. The fog has settled down again, mercifully not quite so thick as before. It was odd the day before yesterday when I was down town on duty to see the crowds round some large windows which had news written up on huge placards.

Personally, I have only seen a couple of French papers since I left England, and they contained simply a repetition of news from the *Daily Mail* before we left England. I feel much better with dry feet; though the boots are coarse, they are strong and useful, but they make me walk like a ploughboy! Still, if the weather gets colder, I can put on a second pair of socks under them. We have been lucky enough to get some good butter and some tinned milk from a small café near here. Of course, we are in the district that is not invaded by the enemy at present. My men are very willing, but very troublesome. They lose themselves and fall out on every pretext.... A Colonel came up yesterday and said: "You back from Aden?"...

I hear a rumour that John is off to India and my brother Kenrick a Major already. He is a lucky fellow! Glad you saw me off on Wednesday at Winchester. I looked up at your window, but could not see you....

[*Note.*—The position of the 1st Battalion Royal Irish Rifles was, at this period of the war, about 20 miles from the town of Ypres, and the billets mentioned in the letters were mostly in and around the little town of Estaires.—F.V.L.]

In Billets.
November 11th, 1914.

I wrote to you last Monday from our camp where we landed. We left that, being put into our train by an old gentleman of your uncle's (Sir John Ross) Brigade. Having told us everything he could, he then went to dinner. In the meantime, we had to put the loaded Army wagons from the ground on to the railway trucks. We finished in about four hours' time, and went off in a very cold train of nearly fifty carriages. Biscuits and tinned meat were distributed to us, and we ran on practically without a stop until 12.30 a.m. Wednesday morning. I say practically, for we halted nearly an hour at one station and got the men some tea. We had no means of washing, so you may imagine we looked like black men in a very short time! Next, we got out of the train and unloaded it in rain, went into some barns and slept until 5 o'clock.... I was in a cart shed much like the one opposite the large barn belonging to the "Park Farm" at Carlton. I had some doubtfully clean straw and my coat and waterproof, but I found it cold all the same. However, as I was only allowed to remain in till 5 a.m., it was not as bad as one might have expected. Marching again at 9 a.m. I went into billets after passing a church badly knocked about by German shells, and a burnt-down house, which owed its departure to the French shells. Here I am in a building very much resembling Willoughby Farm. In the hay barn I have 50 men, 100 men and 11 horses in the stables, and 16 officers in the house, with all the remainder somewhere near me. It is colder and has been blowing a gale up to now, but I expect it will turn to rain again when the wind drops. I was inspected this morning by a superior General: am rather tired of inspections! From where we sit we can see the flash of the shells bursting in front of our position. We hear all sorts of reports as to what is happening. I fancy it is fairly even balanced fighting of a very hard sort. An old lady belonging to the farmer class had her home invaded by the Germans some time ago. They took everything in the house—food, clothes, etc.—and presented her with two francs on leaving, saying they always paid for things! The country is exactly the same as the ground on the opposite side of the Trent without the hedges. I have seen no chateaux or anything of that sort about here. It is evidently a peasant's country. Our men are very funny bargaining with the farmer's wife; now and then we have to come to their assistance over the money question. Rather a curious feature in these parts is that most of the farms have a large wheel for churning attached to the house. A dog is popped into this wheel, and he then has to run for his life, and so does the churning! I suppose such an invention would not be allowed in England on the ground of cruelty nowadays! I am glad to hear that the *Emden* and *Konigsberg* have both been settled. I am only sorry about the ships off Chili. Poor Admiral Cradock! Do you remember him at Dover, when Lord Brassey gave an entertainment to the Fleet?

Well, I think that is all my news. I can hardly keep awake as it is. A pretty cold night, but one just has to put up with it. I only wish that something would happen to end the war with honour to ourselves.

Still it is a mercy to spend a night like this in the house instead of in the trenches. There is no fresh meat in the country, only tinned beef for us!...

In Billets.
November 13th, 1914.

Well, I have not been able to write to you before this, as I try to do every day. Yesterday, for instance, I was up at 5 o'clock, and after an hour's parade, shivering in the dark, I then went off to another, and got back about 1 o'clock. I was instructing my men in the difference between English and French distances—*i.e.*, what 600 yards looked like in this country for rifle ranges, and where an enemy was likely to hide, etc. In the middle of this the Brigade Major dashed up in despair, as some order of his had gone astray. I was wanted to take ten officers at once and to jump into a motor lorry, and go with a party of 30 others to the trenches. I popped my ten officers in, and went off with the Brigade-Major's greatcoat in my hurry! We raced our lorry through country looking just like the Romney Marshes, Sussex. As we went we met refugees flying from a burning town which had been set on fire by German shells. We also passed immense amounts of transports; for troops must live even when they fight. On the way I suddenly saw the back of my last General at D——. You remember him—a very pleasant man. Well, he showed us round the trenches. The shells were bursting up along the forward line held by my brother Hal's[3] old regiment [4th King's Own]. You could see the shrapnel bursting on the ground, and perhaps setting fire to something or other. None of the shells were near us, so we were quite safe. Leaving the line about dark, we had to rattle home. Of course we lost our way, as our maps are on such a small scale, and the inhabitants of one little town told us the wrong direction, mistaking our French, I suppose! But we were not to be done, for we picked up an old lady trotting along in the dark, and, having satisfied her that we were *not* Germans, she soon showed us the road, coming a couple of miles with us. I arrived home—or, rather, at my billet—shivering about 7.30 p.m., having had heavy cold rain during a great part of the day. I turned out to an "Alarm" Parade at 9 o'clock, returning to my house again at 10 p.m. So, you see, I am not eating the bread of idleness! To-day we have all been out and got very wet. It is unpleasant, but one cannot help it in war. I have had very hard work with my returns, and my Quartermaster is getting old. However, I shall rub along now, I trust! To-morrow I am sending my R.C. soldiers to a church with holes in the roof from shells. Don't you think I really deserve well of my Catholic acquaintances, for I have had the priest down twice to see them. Our host tells me that the Germans came here; the people ran away, and that the Germans ran after them, caught eleven, made them dig a big hole in a field, and then shot them. I wonder if it is true. Certainly I have seen some few graves in the fields with no names, just little crosses of rough wood. They may be murdered inhabitants, or they may be simply skirmishers who fell in some inglorious scrap. Please send me a few more packets of plain envelopes; one bundle at a time is quite enough, as I write on this note-book paper; it reduces the amount I have to carry. Some men have been sent to me to be instructed in Machine Guns. What a curious nation we are, training our men quite happily within ten miles of the enemy! I think I told you about our billets in the last letter. The Germans emptied the wine cellar. Imagine an English farm having a wine cellar at all! We do not even burn the wood, and we have done a great trade for these people in milk and butter. Eggs there appear to be none. I expect we shall be moving shortly; but where to I cannot tell. I was glad to find that the French had not at all exhausted their reserves. For instance, there is in the house here a labourer who is a cavalry soldier. He is 43 years of age, and his category is the next to go. Only your first letters have reached me up to now, but some more are expected in to-morrow evening. The General I met yesterday told me that the Prussian Guards, 15,000 strong, were formed up two nights ago, and were told that they must break through our lines, as their Infantry of the Line had made an attempt to do so and had failed. They tried hard; we heard the guns going. They did not get through, and they showed no disposition to try again yesterday morning, fortunately. It is probable that they suffered very severely. If this goes on, they must stop shortly. Possibly you know more about it all than I do, though, as I have seen no papers; in fact, I am absolutely isolated. It has been raining in torrents, but has now stopped for a minute, and the wind is getting up. Horrid in the trenches, I fancy. Our Protestant soldiers open their eyes at the crucifixes scattered all about the country. I have three in the tiny room which I share with Major B———. My doctor is ill, which is a nuisance. I have not yet heard what the Government gave me for my horse "Goldfinch."

Hope you are not having a dull time. I am; but that cannot be helped. I shall be glad to get through this war with honour and return to England. I have had a dreadful knocking about during the last four months, coming from India and the horrid journey home, etc., etc.

Yours....
G.

Please send enclosed letters to your mother and to Aunt Helen. Love to the children. My two new horses I have called Patrick and Michael.

November 18th, 1914.

Still in my dug-out and just now under shrapnel fire. I have been out this morning, having at last got a doctor, and I have arranged with him to get a little morphia with a trained man, so that my poor fellow badly wounded may die in peace. I had a case of that yesterday, when a man died after 12 hours of great pain with both legs gone, and his was not the only one. I received your letters during the night up to November 9th. I am so glad that the shooting was a success. Tell Faulkner now to shoot the cock pheasants as he gets the opportunity.... I had not time to fill in the game book, so please keep it up for me.... Enclosed is a letter from my mother; it was good of her writing so soon.... She must have had a great deal of trouble and expense rebuilding "Oakfield" since the fire last summer.... I hear that my horse "Khaki" is quite a success and much appreciated at Bayfordbury. I have just had a man shot out of a tree where he was posted as a sentry, protected by sandbags, but our fellows got the man who wounded him, and there is general joy. I am also investigating the case of a civilian who was inside our lines with a pass, and who had a friend who ran away, whilst four German soldiers suddenly popped up and let drive at us. So you see I have my work cut out, what with holding my lines, directing our batteries of artillery where to shoot, arranging for hospitals, answering letters, making sketches, laying telephones, and sending messages to Headquarters, etc., etc.!

In the middle of all this I was shelled, and my clerk fled before the storm as he was writing the returns. I am told to remain here for three days more, unwashed and unshaved! It was so cold last night; I was up most of the time doing business, but in between whiles got a little sleep. To-day I have been seeing to my hospital and the graves, and have a four-hour walk before me to-night with the Engineers. Such a cannonade has been going on in Ypres for the last three days. The roar of cannon is quite continuous. Your watch is keeping most excellent time, by-the-bye. I expect this battle will have a great effect on the war. One wonders how many are being killed in it—poor things!... Please send all you have now for the troops, as I imagine they will want anything and everything to keep out the cold if they can carry it. The Government gave me £70 for "Goldfinch," which was good, I think.

November 20th, 1914.

I am now in the trenches in the snow, and it was very cold indeed last night. Can you picture such conditions, lying out in it after dark? All my poor men feel the change very much, coming from the heat of Aden. However, it is business. We are supposed to go out to-morrow night for three days' rest after six nights in the trenches, during which I have not washed or shaved! Yesterday a bullet pierced our splinter-proof roof. Major W—— had his cap cut by one, greatly to his surprise! I was up half the night with orders, etc., coming in. Whilst I was going round quite a pretty little fight developed. Fifty Germans attacked a few of our men; I stood revolver in hand and watched it, as we gradually drove them back. This morning at daybreak our men are reported to have shot two men of a burying party, so there must have been casualties. Still, one is sorry for the burial party. Their guns are knocking things about here; big guns, too. Our Brigadier, General Lowry Cole, asked me if Mrs. L.C. might write to you about comforts for the troops, and I said certainly. If you have any gloves or waistcoats, send them along, please. We thought our friends had arranged to take away their guns, and for one day we did not see them; then they opened again this afternoon. I shall not be sorry to get relieved to-morrow, when we march all night and go into billets, taking our boots off, which will be a great relief. I have caught several local men inhabitants here and sent them off under escort, since which time "sniping" has gradually decreased. Well, I did not write to you yesterday; was too busy. I am inclined to think that Germany has shot her bolt.

In Trenches.
November 21st, 1914.

Very cold, and more snow—I wonder how we can stand it! Fortunately, the Germans are equally badly off. I have had a chequered life. Last night, after a meagre dinner of tinned beef, I found an officer of the Royal Engineers waiting for me, who announced that he and a party of men had come to put my wire entanglements into order. Having done that, they were to go home. Passing along a deep drain, led by myself, we got to the end of a huge mound of earth. Three of my men popped over it in the dark, within 100 yards of some Germans who were lying down firing at us. Then over went the Sappers, whilst I flew off to see that our own men did not fire on them. Back again to my hole in the ground to put other things "in train." Up at 11.30 p.m. to repulse an attack. That driven off, I rolled up in blankets to shiver until 1 a.m., when messages began to pour in from everywhere as to all sorts of things. Up again at 4, and at 5.30 for good, back to the trenches, followed by five officers who are relieving us. This procession was a walk with stooping heads, bullets raining in through the loopholes, and frantic runs along ditches beside hedges (just like the "shallows" at Carlton). I crawled completely doubled up. Suddenly a sniper would see some part of me showing, and would then let drive at me. I had to duck, and then run like a hare until I got to a bank which gave some protection. Needless to say, my coat and riding things are already in holes. Please send me another large packet of chocolate; the last was much appreciated; also some soup squares.

In Billets.
November 23rd, 1914.

We are back again in billets now. Such a business as it was getting out of the trenches. Of course, my men could not leave until the others were in their places; then they had to change back to their roads through the trenches, practically so narrow that they could not pass without stepping over each other, and these three miles long. Well, the result of all was that, moving off at 4.30 p.m., we collected at a road two miles back at 2 in the morning. Just think of it! There was snow and 15 degrees of frost, and we were awfully cold. We got to our billets about 3 a.m., and the General was in my room at 5 o'clock to see me. I was very tired after my week's work, but I think it was successful. My casualties I am not allowed to state, but they were more than I like to count; also, alas! the number of men killed in action recently.... Well, following on from that, you will quite understand that I had much to think about; funerals, wounded men, rations and everything, shivering with cold the whole time. Then I had to go into my returns, and I was even asked to make up maps and sketches. I believe one of my officers had a bullet through his clothes whilst trying to sketch the enemy's position at night. Still, we did our work. One particular night, for instance, I had four officers—patrols—in the enemy's lines. It cost me one man killed and one man wounded, though I heard that Capt. Stevens died too the day after he was hit, poor fellow! Colonel Napier[4] was not wrong when he said it would be a terrible war, but Germany must surely be very nearly at the end of her tether. After all, I must return my boots, as the pair sent, though quite large enough in an ordinary way, are much too small now that I wear two pairs of socks and do not remove them for a week! Did it ever occur to you how difficult it is to feed 1,000 men in a trench 3 miles long when you can only get in at the ends? It took from 5 p.m. to 10 o'clock to get and give them their teas, and then from 3 a.m. to half-past six to give them their breakfast and their food for the day, whilst all the time the enemy was fighting and shooting, and one had to judge to a nicety where to keep everyone until the rations were issued, so that in case the Germans should suddenly rush us we should have enough to repel them. I wonder where you are now—at Rostrevor or at Carlton—and whether I am fated to get home before Christmas or not. In any case, best of luck....

In Billets.
November 24th, 1914.

Off to the trenches again to-night, and please God we shall not lose so many men as before. I had the clergyman up to-day and Holy Communion administered for officers and men. Quite a lot of the former attended. You remember we were together last at Winchester. What a difference between that day and now!... Then, the most stately pile in the world; here a little room in a French farmer's house, with the table pushed into the corner and a few broken chairs to sit upon. An evil-looking bin stands in the corner containing our rations, a pistol on the mantelpiece, and some boots at the fireplace drying, which latter I hastily removed. However, the service was really just the same as at Winchester, excepting that you were not with me. If anything happens to me on this expedition, I should like that small window looking on our pew, representing the Bishop of York's figure, etc., etc., to be filled in to my memory; and, curiously enough, I think the Penitent Thief always one of the greatest heroes in the Bible; for he must have had enormous faith to believe when he was in such a bad way himself.

The snow is fast melting, and, on the whole, it is much warmer than yesterday. Well, beyond this I have no news to give you, excepting that, of course, though Germany may put up a long fight, yet, in my opinion, she is being strained to death to keep herself going, and I believe that she cannot last long at this rate.

November 25th, 1914.

Back in the trenches, and very busy indeed, as apparently we intend to stay here for some time, and we are doing our best to make them habitable for the winter. Our own dug-out, which was 3 feet deep, we have deepened to 4 feet, but just at this moment the roof beams of Major Baker's half have been carried away, whilst a sniper prevents our getting on the top of the roof to shovel off the earth and renew the beams. Altogether a cheerful problem. However, like many others we shall gradually get this right. I was told that the Germans made a great attack in the afternoon two days ago on the Brigade to our right, but were beaten back. I have warned all my men to be ready for a rush at any time. We made an amusing attack two nights ago with 8 men and one officer, all of whom were wrapped in sheets to avoid being seen in the snow. It took place from one of my trenches. The officer got to the German trench, where a man looked into his face. He fired his revolver at one yard, and his men following dashed forward and fired right and left down the trenches. A great scamper ensued, as you may imagine, and then from each German trench burst out a heavy rifle fire. Our guns were ready, and immediately opened on them in the darkness, and presumably caused the enemy many casualties. I must say that I should never be surprised at the war coming to a sudden conclusion, or for it to last a very long time; but I fancy that a great deal depends upon the result of this battle in Poland. The sniping gentleman is tremendously busy at present, but I hope he will not catch me on my way to luncheon. I have to go there very shortly. You see, I believe they have rifles fixed in clumps, and then they fire them by a sentry pulling a trigger. Of course, the shots are erratic to a certain extent, but they find out from spies where the general line of advance to our trenches is, scour them regularly, and now and then bag someone or other. Last night passed quietly enough; we had our scrap about one o'clock. I was out, but nothing serious happened, I am glad to say. The weather has turned to rain again, and the country is losing the snow, whilst the trenches accumulate the rain and mud badly. Please God this war will soon be over.

In Trenches.
November 26th, 1914.

I thought I might have had a letter from you this mail; however, it has not arrived, worse luck! Last night, while talking with the General, a bullet struck near his head, glancing off a brick wall. You should have seen him jump! My nerves have grown stronger, as I've had a good baptism of them when going about. Our trenches were awful. Yesterday I went round them all, and found everything more or less right. Only my leggings were absolutely plastered above my knees with mud. I think I've hit on a good way, if original, of getting ahead of the mud now, by putting my feet into a bag as soon as I come into my dug-out. This is then drawn up nearly to my waist, and collects any mud that falls off, and saves the place. As one does not walk about in it, only crawls, the bag is better than you would have thought! It is turning cold again, and I suppose we shall have a bad night of it. Yesterday evening we discovered a fast machine gun had been brought up against us, so this afternoon I have been amusing myself and one of our batteries by shelling it, but with what result I cannot say. Great stories of Russian doings on the East of Prussia still come to us. About two months more should, I think, give Germany as much as she can do, with her few remaining soldiers, and they must run down fast in numbers. A man looked into one of my loopholes during the night, and told my men that he was an Engineer mending our wire, and the silly fellows thoroughly believed him. I am *certain* he was a German.

In Trenches.
November 27th, 1914.

I received your letter to-day of November 18th, also your mother's of the 21st, for which many thanks. Last night I was up at 1 a.m., turned out by heavy firing. Fortunately, after a time it died away, as I could not get my guns to work! I heard that the Rifle Brigade also tried the white sheet manœuvre with an officer and 8 men lately, but they tell me the officer is missing. One of mine has been at the enemy's lines during the last two nights; I hope he will be all right. We made no fuss, only just lay and watched them, and heard them chattering and sitting round little fires in the trenches. A bullet came through the ruin which I was in close beside me, but as dozens are flying over and around one all the time, it merely attracted my attention by the fact that it passed through two brick walls and went on its way. This pointed German bullet does strange tricks. For instance, one of them yesterday must have struck something, turned at right angles, and gone on, killing an old soldier of mine by striking him on the left temple, poor fellow! Well, I must close. I expect to get out this evening, if alive. By the way, please send me several pounds of plum pudding—the richer, the better. We can stand it. Very greedy thinking about things to eat, but it takes one's mind off more serious affairs. Young McClintock's regiment (the Gordon Highlanders) has been sent in alongside myself. I went down to see it, but Stanley was not there.

In Billets.
November 28th, 1914.

It is very odd, but all your letters have not arrived. We moved out of trenches in the dark last night, and as we got well away were feeling ourselves safe. "Zip" came a bullet, and hit the ground beside me; it seemed rather unfair when one thought one was well out of range. We got in here at 8.30 p.m., and, having two cold pheasants sent by Major B.'s brother, we supped sumptuously. Please send me some more pheasants or partridges cooked as before, and sewn up in sacking. This house is a farm much like that one on the road to Newark before you reach Muskham Bridge. The owner is evidently a rich man, for everything is very nice, electric light laid on, but unfortunately not going! We had our rest rudely disturbed by the Germans trying to shell us. Whether we were betrayed by people pretending to be refugees or not I cannot say, but within an hour of sending two away the shelling commenced. Fortunately they missed us, though I heard that a couple of officers of another regiment were killed. A possible reason, however, which we have since found out is that some heavy guns of our own have placed themselves beside us, thus letting us in for all the shells that miss the enemy. We are rather irate at it. But to return to our house. It has six bedrooms on the first floor, and some attics; the rooms are quite middle-class looking, though the furniture in the dining-room is of nice walnut. The Germans looted the place and smashed the mirrors over the mantelpiece, whilst there is a bullet hole through the door. I sincerely hope that something will happen shortly to bring home to the German nation what a thing it is to invade another country's property. It is quite *pitiful* to see the way everything is knocked about. The china in the house is in the pretty French style, the coffee pot particularly neat and nice. It is curious sitting here with shells having fallen all round us within 300 yards, and yet to be so perfectly peaceful. Still, it is war. I said to one of my captains: "Where did you bury So-and-So yesterday?" and he replied: "Where he was shot, sir. He was a heavy man, and we could not take him to the place where we buried the others." So there the poor man lies in a ploughed field, and no more trace of him excepting that in his humble way he did his duty and gave his life for his country. I suppose the evening of November 30th will see us in the trenches again. By the way, please tell Miss P―― that I have found her handkerchief most useful in the trenches. Nothing smaller would have been any good at all. I am trying to get my chestnut horse back, and asking the Brigade Major to telegraph for him to the Remount. The Government has commenced to issue to the men goatskin coats of white and brown or black goats. Where such a goat lives I do not know; anyhow, here is his skin! I suspect I shall very soon have one too, if the weather gets colder.

In Billets.
November 29th, 1914.

You can see by this that your notepaper has duly arrived, for which I am much obliged. I was also glad to get your letter, and I am sure that you must be very pleased to be back in Rostrevor again. Curious how I have been kept away from you for three years, is it not, first by my promotion, and then this awful war.... Well, yesterday I think I told you that I saw a shell strike close beside one of my companies, so I ran and put the men into bomb-proof, or rather splinter-proofs. Having seen they were safe, I went on with my work, though it is not pleasant doing this sort of thing whilst shells are flying about! Anyhow, I started out afterwards to reconnoitre the road to a certain town, and passed two men of the Rifle Brigade making a coffin. I asked for whom it was intended, and found that this same shell had killed a very nice Major, called "Harman," of the Rifle Brigade, whilst another man was badly wounded, and a Captain also in the Rifle Brigade. It all happened just as far from me as Carlton Village is from the house, or a few yards more at farthest. Well, we buried the poor fellow after dark. This morning we had service both for our Catholic and Church of England men, and after that the General decided to inspect my regiment. As he approached, so did the shells, and in a few seconds everyone was flying for shelter to ditches and holes in the ground like rabbits to their burrows. Having knocked us about with 300-lb. shells, they then thought that we should be out of the house, and they let loose with shrapnel, which is a great man-killer. I watched the first burst coming, and had everyone under cover whilst they rained this around. I think they must have been in a bad humour. At all events, they wasted £500 worth of ammunition to no purpose. I expect they are told by spies which houses we occupy, as they appeared to follow us about steadily. It has become much milder, but still cold enough when we turn out at five o'clock in the morning. One certainly does not eat the bread of idleness in the British

Army at present! Here comes our solitary lamp, borrowed from the absent farmer, but before it arrives we must close the blinds, as the light would certainly insure a shelling for us. I am glad you had a good run across to Ireland, and that Sydney was a good boy. I wonder how much longer we are going to stay here. Rumour has it that the enemy is moving back, but I cannot say.

In Billets.
November 30th, 1914.

We are still in billets and still under a heavy fire; a nasty cold rain is falling, and altogether it is very disagreeable, excepting that it would be worse in the trenches, as being *more* cold and wet. Well, last night we discovered a pigeon loft in the ruined part of the town, and as we have orders to destroy all these birds we put a guard on it, and Major B—— and I walked down to the Brigade office and asked if we could kill the lot. We found, however, that it was supposed to belong to the French Army, so we returned sorrowfully home. On our way we had a near shave, for out of the darkness whizzed a shrapnel shell. I heard it coming, having very quick ears, and shouted "Down!" It was rather amusing to see what happened. The three men stood stock still, and gazed like owls solemnly into the dark. Major B ... walked rapidly forward in the direction he was then going, whilst I gave a flying jump and was face downward in orthodox style in a second and into a ditch. The shrapnel landed its contents within 20 yards of us, but all escaped unhurt, I'm thankful to say. We managed to get under cover before the next one came. Such is our life here, though we are politely said to be resting! It is fairly raining shrapnel 200 yards up the road now, but what I am on the look-out for are high-explosives, as they are so much more dangerous to troops amongst buildings. The other day, on November 9th, we heard a tremendous burst of firing, and in *The Times* of November 23rd I see it is thought that the British guns caught the German reserves forming up for an attack on us, and destroyed them in large numbers. Certainly, as Colonel Napier says, it is an awful war. However, I notice that a lot of German fuses do not explode their shells, which makes me think they have not got quite so good a supply of stuff as they try to make us believe! I want very much to go out, but, on the whole, I think it is safer to stay in at present. Sir John Ross will have his work cut out to write the history of the Coldstream Guards for this war.

My mind is so full at present that I cannot say if I shall be able to write ours, even if I come through all right. However, I keep an official war diary, which will always help greatly. These brutes have now changed from shrapnel to high explosives, which are whirling over our heads and bursting in the town about 400 yards farther down. I hope they will not drop one short and put it in here, which would be good-bye to all of us....

LETTERS OF DECEMBER, 1914.

In Trenches.
December 2nd, 1914.

My Dear F——

Am sitting in my dug-out scrawling this by the light of a signaller's lamp. I was awake at 4.30 a.m., working hard practically ever since, and it is now dark with a beautiful moon rising. I have been very busy trying to get ahead of a German trench which they had sapped up to us. We arranged to have it stormed by Capt. O'Sullivan and Mr. Graham, but as the Royal Engineers could not let me have an officer to put a mine in just then, it had to be postponed for one day; and that brings us out of our trenches, as we are supposed to go into rest billets to-morrow night. Well, I have now settled that a battery of Field Artillery is to fire on them at fixed hours during the night, and Mr. T—— has been sent down there with his machine gun, so it is quite on the cards that we shall have a merry evening! I hear the guns opening as I write, and wonder if our friends, who greatly outnumber us, will rush us to-night or not. If they knew how very weak we were, I expect they would try!

I forgot to tell you that I was ordered to send away a Major, and consequently Major Alston had to go to the 2nd Battalion with two other officers. During my rounds this morning with the General he incautiously exposed himself, and he was instantly fired at, the bullet striking between us as we stood about a yard apart. Also, two minutes after I had finished shaving early in the day, a bullet came through the place breaking the pane of glass. Such is Providence, and you see that, so looked after, it is as safe here as in England, if it is our Lord's will.... Your Mother sent me a second paper to fill in. It is curious to be a Trustee and do such work in the trenches. The sniping that is going on now is perfectly deafening.

Yours....
G——.

In Trenches.
December 3rd, 1914.

We go out of the trenches to-night, and after marching six miles to try and avoid the German shells we shall all put up at a small town where for the first time since November 10th we shall not be under fire, and when we shall have the opportunity of taking off our boots and sleeping without them, also for the first time since we left our port of landing on November 7th. The poor Colonel I took this dug-out from was killed last week, as I saw by the papers. He was a nice sensible man. I shall not be sorry to get out to-night and into bed for a change. My sleep yesterday was from 12 midnight to 5 a.m., and I was awakened three times to answer messages. No chance of any more during the 24 hours before or after. By the way, a story that happened quite lately might amuse you. An old Frenchwoman came to a house occupied by our cooks, and asked whether she might get some clothes out; for all the houses are deserted by the inhabitants. She presented a recommendation, obviously written in English by a foreigner. We thought her suspicious, detained her, took the permit, and sent her away without allowing her in. We cannot arrest her, as the Staff will not let us do so. Well, she then came and found out where the observation station of the heavy artillery was, and was seen to go into the building opposite, take some clothes, and come out, shutting the door and fastening the shutters; this marked the house, and she had not been gone 20 minutes when four shells landed together and blew the place to pieces, just missing the observation post! Of course she was a spy for the Germans, who watched from a church some distance off through a telescope, and so were shown where the station was. Then the guns opened on our cooks, but passed them, knocking down a wall alongside. Curious that we are not allowed to intern these people; but the French authorities object. Probably many messages are sent to the Germans by underground wires.

G.B.L.

P.S.—The last of this note is rather disjointed, but that is because I have been giving a learned dissertation on the best means of circumventing a German sap approaching us.

In Billets.
December 4th, 1914.

We left our trenches yesterday without regret, and retired some six miles way to a little country town about the size of Newry, where we are quartered, or rather billeted, for a couple of days before we go back again to our diggings. The exchange had to be done in the dark, and I got the regiment away without casualties, which was better than the night we went in, when I lost two men killed. It is strange being out of fire for the first time for three weeks, and nobody being killed or wounded beside one at present! Also it seems funny to see people walking again in the streets, and to hear children's voices, instead of only soldiers dodging from house to house whilst these latter are falling to pieces about their ears and all around them. Your things duly arrived, and are at this moment being distributed to the men, and are much appreciated by them, excepting the chest protectors, which I suspect they will not wear! I am glad you have done so well with the plum-pudding fund for the Regiment. Your Mother's offering was *most* generous, and Aunt E——'s too. We came out of the trenches by creeping down ditches, and then assembled at a place a mile away in the moonlight, and we stole cautiously along, leaving gaps between us, so that if we were shelled we should only lose a certain number. Many of the men could hardly stand, their feet were so numbed with the cold of the trenches, but we got them safely in about 10 p.m., and they are sleeping in all sorts of queer places. One lot are in a granary four stories high. There is only one ladder, so it will take nearly half an hour to get four hundred men out of the building. By-the-bye, you might tell Sir John Ross of a feat done by a Russian bullet which I would not have believed possible. The bullet struck one of our rifle barrels. Of course the distance was only 400 yards, but it cut clean through the massive steel barrel as if it had been butter! I know that it always takes four feet of earth to stop it. I have to go over now to dine with our Divisional Commander, General Davis. It seems so odd getting a night off like this. Khaki dress, of course. It was not my Brigade which did the bayonet charge; when that occurs, you will see the casualty list will be full of killed and wounded officers of this Regiment, I am afraid. It was my old Battalion, the 2nd R.I.R.

P.S.—I hear that my old friend Capt. Kennedy was amongst them, and died from his wounds. I am so sorry.

G.B.L.

In Billets.
December 5th, 1914.

No letters to-day. Report says that the Germans have blown the railway up, but I do not think so. It is much more probable that one of the bridges has broken through overwork. As a matter of fact, they did blow up some bridges at the beginning of the war, and the French had to put in temporary ones, and these are most likely giving way now. It is very cold, with hail and sleet. I should think the trenches will be worth seeing when we go back to them to-morrow. I only wish the war was over, but one has to put up with these things. I see from your letter that you are sending us a plum pudding from Rostrevor House. If this is so, please thank your aunt for her kindness. It will be well received. As to the comforts for the men, those you sent by post have arrived, but not all coming through the forwarding officer. In any case, they are amply supplied now, and only require things which are not given by Government, such as gloves, cigarettes and matches, and the two latter they often get from friends. I had a gigantic consignment from the York Street Linen Mills in Belfast, and wrote to thank the directors. Please send me a cake of Toilet Soap, Pears or any sort will do—not too big—if it will go in my soap box. I had a pleasant little dinner last night on Ration Beef at the General's. He told me, with regard to the shooting of General Delarey in S. Africa, that it was now said the Government out there meant to shoot Beyers as well, as they were both supposed to be in the swim to raise a rebellion, but I cannot believe it. The other guest was Col. Wedderburn, who is the Hereditary Standard Bearer of Scotland, and is in charge of a Militia Battalion out here. He is a very nice fellow too. I am off to try to see General Keir of the 6th Division.

In Billets.
December 6th, 1914.

I have had the Regiment at church, and now I am dashing off a note to you before I change and get into my old clothes. You will be glad to hear that Sir John's chamois leather waistcoat fits me quite well. I tried it on here, because it is "unhealthy" to stand up in the trenches. I went over yesterday and saw Gen. Keir, whom I served under in South Africa. He commands a Division in this war, and is another old friend of mine, like General Inglefield. The road I took was paved with cobble stones in the middle, and on each side was a sea of mud, a specimen of what they are like about here, as there is no stone in the country, only clay. It was very nice getting out on horseback again for ten or twelve miles, even along such a road as that. All the French farmhouses have more artistic fronts than ours; smart shutters, etc., give them an imposing appearance, but it begins and ends there fairly well, I think! The town in which we are is the same as a poor part of Belfast might be—a long paved street; mean houses, and shops on either side, with dirty little slums running off to the right and left. Then here and there you come to a better class of house looking rather out of proportion. I suppose these are the remains of the old ones, when it was a village occupied by some prosperous doctor or tradesman. However, I have not been able to find out if there are any gentry in the place. Our hostess is the widow of a French officer, but she appears to live in the kitchen! I asked the Mess sergeant whether the French people did anything curious in their cooking, and he at once said, "Yes; they never eat any meat, only vegetables and pork!" Our Divisional General, a Guardsman who is a great stickler for everything being quite right, was horrified the other day when crossing a bridge to see a Special Reserve sentry of the "Black Watch" with his rifle between his knees and his face buried in a bowl of soap. Of course, his job was to watch the bridge and to present arms to the

General. So the latter sternly asked him if he was the sentry, and he received the affable reply: "I am; and I am vera cold." History does not relate any more! Well, I must give you my best wishes with my present for Christmas. It seems a long time off yet, but you know how slowly the post goes. I really think I have had no letters from anyone since I arrived here excepting yourself.

In Trenches.
December 7th, 1914.

I am sorry to tell you that on the way to the trenches we lost poor Captain Allgood, whom you will remember. I had ordered everyone to return, wished them good luck, and was waiting to see that they were all in whilst the Germans were sniping us, when someone came and reported to me that a man had been shot through the shoulder by the same bullet which I afterwards heard was believed to have killed Capt. Allgood. The stretcher-bearers brought the latter in, and I sent for the doctor at once, but he could only pronounce him to be dead also! He was shot through the heart, and fell down remarking: "I am hit, but I am all right," and never spoke or moved again. He leaves one little daughter and his young wife. I did not like taking him out here on account of his being married, and now he really has been killed. I have just written to his wife, though I have never seen her. Still, that is part of a Colonel's business. Poor Capt. Allgood! He looked so peaceful lying on the stretcher. We are rather miserable in the trenches, as we have to live in a sea of mud. I think it is worse this time than ever. I have been busy getting it shovelled out and trying to cheer everyone up. Yesterday when we were coming in, the Germans started shelling the village we had to go through. I moved round it by another road and saved my men, and sent a message to the G.O.C. saying that I had been obliged to do this. Last night I received a telegram from Sir Henry Rawlinson that the Germans were expected to attack. They did not, fortunately, but they are now playing on us with their machine guns. So we are very busy! A cheerful life!

In Trenches.
December 9th, 1914.

Just a line to try and keep up my regular custom of writing to you every day whenever I can! A shell descended yesterday in the cottage I run across to for my meals. I had just left, but I fancy there were still enough people on the spot to be badly frightened. The Guard over me from the Lincoln Regiment all fell or were blown down by the explosion. Little Mr. Wright also was surprised. However, only Major Baker's servant was hurt by a blow from a broken tile which cut his chest, and another man was hit by a flying brick. After that I was showing the General and other celebrities round the trenches. In one place they really had a most amusing time, running down a very muddy ditch crouched up double, whilst stray bullets flew about, and the shell burst fortunately just 200 yards beyond us. Nasty stuff, too; a tree about 50 feet high was caught by the explosion and cut off just half way up. We go back to our shell-swept area for 3 days, though whether we are much safer there I do not know, but we certainly are more comfortable. Here with the rain there has been a steady drip into the dug-out, and added to this the trenches have fallen in, and they, of course, are ankle deep in mud. Mud is everywhere; on my face, on my coat, and up nearly to my waist. I hear that the hostess of our last billets turned rusty with the next people, and refused to let them into her house, so had to come under the correction of the Provost Marshal. I thought she would get into trouble. Your postcard was very amusing. I heard from General Macready[5] two days ago. The guns are booming away, but the sniping has decreased to-day.

I have to stop for duty now....

In Billets.
December 10th, 1914.

We marched away from our trenches last night, and no one was hit, fortunately. A machine gun opened on us just before we started, and gave three bursts of fire, and of course the sniping went on steadily as usual. I soon found out that this gun fire was drawn by a foolish corporal of the Lincolnshire Regiment, who, in cooking his guards' suppers, had a fire with flames four feet high. A few biting words relieved my feelings and put the fire down! Still bullets did fly around us, over our heads and beside us, while we passed along in the black night. Mr. Wright, my Adjutant, saw one strike in a puddle between him and myself as we marched at the head of the Regiment. You will be interested to know what our 72 hours in the trenches cost us. Of course I cannot tell you our casualties for fear this letter should be read by the enemy, but if you remember the number of our house in Victoria Park, Dover, and General H——'s combined, that was the amount of my killed and twice that of my wounded;[6] so you see what a business it all is. Please God the Germans will shortly have had enough. I used to say that they were losing a quarter of a million men every fortnight. Now, however, it has turned out that mine was an under-estimate, and that they are really losing 300,000 a fortnight, more than I gave them credit for. People thought me over-sanguine, but now they say I am rather a good judge. We have just heard the news of the naval battle off the Falkland Islands this morning, and we are very elated. My idea is that Germany's frantic attacks on the Russians and on ourselves here will wear her out faster even than if we attacked; and "it will arrive," as the French say, that she will be so done that she will have to surrender at discretion, because her population will fight no longer. I wonder whether Sir John agrees with my views. Personally, I think it surprising that Bavaria has gone on as long as she has. I fancy that she will be the first of the German Federals to jib. Your letter of the 1st arrived whilst I was writing this, also a joint letter from Hal and Blanche; I was so glad to get all three. As to clothes, I keep an old suit for the trenches; when I get out and have to go anywhere, I turn out quite smartly, excepting that my boots and leggings are "dubbed" with grease instead of being polished. When my old suit is done, my form will be encased in Government khaki garments with my badges of rank transferred, and that will keep me going to the end of the war.

I hope you thanked Mrs. Horsborgh[7] for the donation to the Regiment on my behalf. It was very little I was able to do for her husband beyond burying him, but it was a kind thought of hers. The chamois leather waistcoat is the comfort of my life, thanks to Sir John, and the idea of another plum pudding from Aunt Blanche is already making us feel better. I had my first tub since I came across to-day. I think it was a pig-tub, but I had it cleaned out and washed.

G.B.L.

In Billets.
December 11th, 1914.

I received three letters from you yesterday. Two of December 4th, and one of the 1st inst. Likewise to-day a cake from Rostrevor House, for which many thanks from all of us, not forgetting to thank the cook! We wolfed half of it at luncheon, and the remainder is to grace our tea-table, when we have asked the two staff officers of the Brigade to come. I have just been out on a circuitous route to see my transport, which lies about 2-½ miles behind the town where I am billeted at present, just out of the range of any shells. I took a ride round to see how the country lay, riding hard with my heart in my mouth where there was any chance of fire, and sauntering along whenever it appeared to be safe. As a matter of fact, one hardly knows where to expect a shell. Three miles from this battery the other day shrapnel burst within 20 yards of me. Ten yards nearer, and I would, humanly speaking, have been done. Well, now as to your kind gift of a sheepskin coat and gloves, I am afraid I cannot keep them, for there are no means of carrying them, unfortunately. As a matter of fact, much as

I should like them, all these things mean so many pounds extra kit. I am only allowed 50 lbs. in weight, so when you have taken into account a heavy pair of boots, one's blankets and valise, second coat, and riding breeches, there is really no room for more. I have to see that everyone does not exceed 35 lbs. (I, being the Colonel, am allowed 15 lbs. more kit), but I cannot in honour exceed my weight. I keep wondering whether we are likely to move forward shortly. I fancy that our German friends are being shaken up by Russia, whilst I am sure it is a question of time when Hungary goes for Austria. In great haste.

December 12th, 1914.

Last night was a red-letter day, for two plum puddings arrived from Rostrevor House, and also the refill for my battery before the old one ran out, so I am quite happy as to that point now. I have also written to Aunt B——. Many thanks for the figs. Isn't it strange how one always becomes a child again when one gets on a campaign and requires food of all sorts like a schoolboy, though the Government gives quite enough, and good solid food too. I had a parcel from Aunt H—— yesterday, with one of her usual kind letters; I seized the woollen cap for myself, and I am quite sure it is much better for sleeping in in the trenches than the muffler you knitted for me, as the ends always get entangled in the mud of that rather dreadful place. By the way, when you have time, please send me a piece of shaving soap. I have stuck to shaving steadily, and propose doing so unless you want me to grow a beard! I was very much surprised when, after seven days without being able to shave, to see my face come out perfectly black all over! I thought I was fair, so apparently my moustache is a fraud! Is it not funny?

In Trenches.
December 13th, 1914.

We marched out to the trenches with very little firing, and found that the whole of them were more or less full of water. While visiting one company last night about 5.45 a.m. I had to wade through water just below the top of my leggings. What that means by remaining afterwards in wet boots I leave you to judge. I managed to get mine changed at 11 a.m., as I had a dry pair of socks in my holsters, and put my feet back into the wet boots. In one place which I have not yet walked through, the water is actually up to the waist. One sergeant of the Lincoln Regiment was left for us to dig out, as he was hopelessly bogged when his regiment had to march away; whilst another man was pulled out by main force and left his boots behind him, and after walking a mile in bare feet was put into a cart. The enemy have had the audacity to open on us with a machine gun, and spent last night with it trying to shoot down my principal communication trench, so, as I have more or less placed the gun, I am asking the artillery to fire on it without delay. A curious way of spending the third Sunday in Advent, shivering with cold in a dug-out, with lots of bullets humming overhead, but not so many shells just at present. The men and officers are having a bad time, but war is never pleasant.

P.S.—The sequel to the maxim gun fire is that one of my men has been knocked down and hit in the leg, in the arm, and back of the head. The fact being that he was going for water, and finding the ditch very dirty, foolishly jumped out, and was promptly knocked over at once. The enemy is now shelling over our heads most cheerfully. One wonders when all this will stop....

G.B.L.

In Trenches.
December 14th, 1914.

Here I am in my dripping dug-out, even more so than usual. The water is up to my waist in some places. Things are moving, I think, and perhaps our friends the Germans may shortly move also. We have been pouring shells on the poor dears all day. This morning I was lucky in getting hold of a German helmet. The Divisional General has been screaming for one for days, as we wish to find out what troops are in front of us. I have had patrols prowling about everywhere at nights trying to catch a prisoner. Yesterday morning, for a wonder, we found some Germans patrolling outside their trenches, and fired upon them, but they got away. This was just at daybreak; but, going very carefully over the ground as soon as we could in the dark, we came upon a helmet, either dropped in flight, or else one of the men had been hit. However, we carried it off in triumph, and so found out for the General what he wanted to know. Thanks for your news. As to poor Mr. Innes Cross of our regiment, who is missing, I know nothing. The other or 2nd Battalion might tell you something. A machine gun has been going hard at my trench for some time, off and on....

In Trenches.
December 15th, 1914.

It was our evening to go off to the town six miles away for the three days in every twelve, which we get to steady our nerves, I suppose.

Unfortunately, some other operations had to be carried out, so we were not able to leave, after all, and we are still here, worse luck! I was summoned this morning to go up a road to meet the General. I found him in a farm, having been obliged to take cover from rifle fire. After the business was settled, I saw him off to comparative safety, and then trudged back to our trenches, meeting a stretcher with one of our men shot through the chest below the heart when he was on the road, also on duty. I will say this for the men, that whilst I go off duty with my heart in my mouth and hurry through it, they saunter about, and no amount of checking will make them understand that it is dangerous to idle about in the open. Afterwards they are hit—if not seriously wounded. They are very like little children, rather annoyed, but in their hearts, I am sure, secretly glad that they have escaped from the awful squalor of the trenches to the comparative comfort of a wounded man in hospital. It is turning a little colder now, which will be really a great improvement over the sloppy weather we have been having. My headquarters are being moved from my awful dug-out to a house, or rather cottage, where I shall not feel the cold quite so much; but I sincerely hope that the enemy will not find out where I am, as they will then shell me out of existence! I must close now to get ready to move....

In Trenches.
December 16th, 1914.

As I told you in yesterday's letter, I have moved my headquarters back 400 yards, so now I am about 700 yards behind the firing line, and something like 1,100 yards from the Germans. We are in a house of sorts which has mysteriously escaped being destroyed. It is protected by a barn more or less ruined, and so the bullets miss it, and also the shells, though they burned a building within four yards of us. This is the house near by which I saw five shells burst the first day I came up here. It was most weird last night as I was lying on the floor to hear bullet after bullet strike the wall; one has come through the window, but that was unusual. When the native troops were in here, they lost three men killed at the front door, but I think we have polished off that sniper since then. Sometimes the bullets glance off the brickwork with a shower of sparks. It is very unhealthy to go out on either side of the farmhouse. I went my rounds yesterday in the evening. Such a time I have never had! Imagine going along a trench just wide enough for your shoulders; your head up to the original level of the ground, and the earth piled up on either side for two or three feet; the bottom was soft mud with water well above the knees. One sank into this whilst one struggled on, carrying revolver or rifle. In my case, revolver strapped on, and holding up my cloak to prevent it getting under my feet in my dreadful flounders. Several times I nearly stuck for good, but just managed to get through. I succeeded in putting on dry things afterwards, but the men, I am sorry to say, could not do so. I asked the doctor to go and inspect this morning, and see if there was anything he could suggest. He went off cheerfully enough, but came back two hours later a dirtier, if a wiser, man, and his only remark to me was: "Well, it will not last. No men could stand that very long!" I replied that we *must* do so longer than the Germans. The pheasants duly arrived, and we are grateful as ever. I have written to your Mother.

G.B.L.

There is a big fight going on to our left about fifteen miles away.

In Trenches.
December 17th, 1914.

You are safely in Carlton, I trust, by now. I am afraid I wish I was there, too, in one sense, though certainly not in another. The war was none of our seeking, but it has got to be seen through by anything that calls itself a soldier! What I feel is the constant discomfort, not to mention the danger; of the latter there is no doubt, and our trenches are right to the fore. We had quite enough of it yesterday with rifle bullets. To-day they varied the entertainment by putting big shells about us, fortunately not on us, so our battery had to change its position. Of course, we, the infantry, must hold our ground, and cannot move.... Enclosed is the Special Order of the Day[8]; perhaps you would like to keep it. I am having a luncheon party to-day to eat the pheasants and plum pudding. It consists of Col. MacAndrew and one of his officers who have come up the road from the headquarters of the Lincoln Regiment, which is on our right. The guns are shooting cheerfully again over our heads, but I am feeling very fit, having just had a hot tub—the first for some time. Your French postcard was returned to me by the stupid post, so I shall try and send it to you in an envelope, as you want to keep it for a curiosity. Many thanks for the turkey. I do not see why you should worry so much to send me things, ... but it is most good of you. Thanks for mittens; I think everyone here is now more or less supplied; but mine made by you will be much esteemed. I am sorry that your cousin, Sir Standish Roche, has gone and that S——— will now be a widow. I must close.

I do not think any of us can get away on leave at present, and if we could, I hardly like leaving the men in the trenches.

G.B.L.

In Trenches.
December 18th, 1914.

We are at present apparently preparing for some adventure or other! One never knows how these affairs will turn out. This is indeed the most trying of wars; our life is one of incessant fighting. My experience of last night will illustrate the sort of thing that goes on. I wanted to go round my trenches, but a party of recruits came in just at that time; one was hit on the road half a mile back. He, poor fellow! was taken to hospital, and will probably be in England within ten days of leaving it. So I saw them away, and started to follow them up. I then dived down into a ditch and staggered along, my boots covered with foul mud and water, whilst a sniper commenced to try and take the trench I was in; enfilade it, they call it. Well, I went farther on up the ditch, getting worse and worse into the mire right over my knees. The mud actually worked its way through my leggings to my skin. I wandered on, heavy sniping hissing over my head or into the parapet, covering me with clay occasionally. Of course, everyone who lives in these particular trenches has wet feet day and night. Having been round and talked to everybody and done my best to cheer them up, I met and had a word with Capt. Rodney. He remarked: "Do not stay where you are, sir, I beg of you, for my servant was shot and killed just on that spot, and another man was wounded by the same bullet." It went clean through a book that the unfortunate man was reading. So I discreetly toddled, or rather waded, home about midnight. This morning one of my men was shot through the lungs, not far from our room, and he died at once. This just shows you what a time we go through here, always having to keep our eyes open! Poor Capt. Whelan was killed, I saw in yesterday's paper. He had been lent to the Royal Irish Regiment. Well, good-bye....

In Trenches.
December 19th, 1914.

This morning your kind present of ginger cake, plum pudding, and mittens, also soap, arrived, for all of which many thanks. You will be interested to hear what was going on last night, which I did not like to tell you at the time I was writing. We had been summoned in the morning to receive the General's order for an attack on a trench by the Rifle Brigade. The real attack, however, was to be made by someone else on quite another part of the line. We were to demonstrate. Well, if you ever heard Hell let loose, it was whilst I was writing that letter. Probably over fifty guns took part in it, and the firing was quite close overhead. It may have been 100 guns really—some very heavy ones. Then about 10 miles of trenches were blazing away at the Germans, and they were blazing back at us. Bullets were racing through our roof, and there I sat in a little room, shivering with cold for we could light no fire. I was not allowed to go into my firing line, but sat near the two telephones connecting me with the Artillery and with my own Regiment. A reinforcement of some Territorials was sent to help us. We finished up by capturing the trenches and also some prisoners, while the Rifle Brigade then went off to the trench that they visit occasionally, and there found a German who had been dead for about a fortnight. This was the net result of the little engagement; but it was very long drawn out at the time. In the morning, when the troops returned, the Germans caught the company moving with shell, and only that Major Baker and myself flew for our lives and hurried people about, we should have lost a lot. I have seldom used worse language! It had its comic side, too, for several of the men got so frightened that they fell into a cesspit in trying to take cover, and two were knocked over and wounded. It is very nasty having shell whistling over your head and bursting all around. At the present moment our batteries have opened again, but nothing like the business of last night. Two more of my fellows were badly hit at the same time, and I had to send a man to give them morphia while awaiting the doctor. Another near squeak was a bullet striking beside me from a glancing shot where I was standing, as I thought, in absolute safety. I am enclosing you a letter from Mrs. Allgood; she is a plucky woman. I had a very nice letter from Sir J—— R——— The bombardment of Scarborough was a cruel affair. Now the country will have to see it through....

Dear Mrs. Laurie,

I have made a great effort, as I cannot draw, to produce a Christmas card for you; it is the house (?) that the Colonel and I live in! Very old, and much knocked about by a shell in part of the roof, and bullet holes through it and both the windows, as I have endeavoured to show. In times of peace it is a very small public house, 3 rooms and a garret in which I live. The Colonel is very well, and seems to enjoy plodding knee-deep through the mud in the trenches. The Germans roused us this morning by dropping pieces of shell on our little house. We have just lunched off a most excellent turkey which you sent; it was splendid.

I hope men do not get mud fever like horses; if so, we ought to do so!

I trust that the war will have come to an honourable end before many months, and that we may all meet again.

With very best wishes for 1915.

Yours very sincerely,
W. CLINTON BAKER.

In Trenches.
December 20th, 1914.

I heard that our people of the 2nd Battalion were driven out of the trenches by bombs from the Germans, with a loss of 8 officers and 200 men, but that may be one of the many yarns always spread about this sort of show. We have just this moment received a report that an attack is expected on us towards 4 p.m. It is now after 3 o'clock, and we have had to hurry indeed to get things ready. This morning, after our standing to arms, which always takes place at five o'clock, the Germans opened on us with heavy and moderate guns. The first shell sent the fuse through my roof, the next knocked a brick in at the side of the wall, and then I jumped out and started putting the men into covered ditches. We had between 50 and 100 shells thrown at us within three-quarters of an hour, but fortunately no one was hit. All the time, of course, rifle fire went on as usual. Such was our Advent Sunday's amusement, and the shelling continued intermittently during the whole of the morning. Our trenches are a perfect bog; I shall find some difficulty in getting round them to-night even if we are not driven out of them. As to the shelling of the East Coast, you should see what these places look like after the enemy gets through with them, for their guns (howitzers) fire nearly as large shells as warships do from their guns. The man who brought the message to me was blown off his bicycle as he came along by four shells bursting and knocking down two or three houses beside him, two miles to the rear of us. Life is too awful for description out here now, and the men feel desperate at times. Whether the Germans are equally badly off I do not know, but there is little doubt that they must be; still, they are such a disciplined nation that it is difficult to see where the first break will come, excepting that as Germany consists in reality of several nations put together, the smaller ones may think it worth while to break off from the Empire and to make terms for themselves. My opinion is that Hungary will shortly do this. By the way, what we thought was another plum pudding turned out to be your turkey, and it was voted the best one we ever tasted! Many thanks for it and the pheasants, which also arrived this morning....

In Trenches.
December 21st, 1914.

Your letter of December 15th, in which you said that you had got back to Carlton, arrived last night. I wish I could run across and see you, but it will be hard for me to get a fortnight just now like your cousin Massereene. You see, he is Cavalry, and attached to the Staff Headquarters of the Division; so also is Percy Laurie. Major S. McClintock got leave, so I hope mine will come in due course, but even then I am not sure I can leave my men. I think I told you in my letter last night that we received a frantic message from our Brigadier-General to expect an attack at 4 p.m. As a matter of fact, there was less fighting than usual, and I lost fewer men. My night's experiences were almost humdrum! Leaving my ruin at 9.15 p.m., accompanied by my bugler and clad in my old waterproof, I sallied out and ran the gauntlet of some snipers from the German lines, then dived into my ditch, floundered up it in mud for about a quarter of a mile, perhaps more, secured some Engineers I have at last got hold of to improve the place, went on, saw Major Wright and Capt. Tee, both as deaf as possible from cold, etc. The water was steadily rising in their trenches, and had already flooded their dug-out; another one had fallen in, whilst their third was leaking badly; so, on the whole, they were not in a good way. Then I struggled on through the mud round the trenches, seeing that men were awake, that necessary digging was being carried out, that lights were not showing, that sentries were posted at proper points, and that officers visited them regularly; for all have to keep to their particular business in this horrible time. I got back to my ruins about 12.30 a.m., having sent a message to the gunners that some of their shells were pleasantly going into my trenches in the darkness, and not into the enemy's. By twenty minutes to 1 o'clock I had dry boots and garments on, and, wrapping myself in blankets, was fast asleep, despite artillery fire and infantry fighting on my right. I awoke at 3 o'clock, went round again, saw everything was right, then to sleep once more until 5.15 a.m., when I was up for good. It is a hard life. To-night we take two companies back to just outside rifle fire, the first time for ten days, though well within shell fire. We have only been out of that for three days since we came into trenches on November 15th. I have had various family letters which I hope to answer in time. Heard, or rather Major B—— did, from Lord Grenfell. I had sent him some message.

He says that he thinks the Turks will not invade Egypt; but the great question in Russia which alone prevents this nation from crushing the German Army at once is the single line of railway that brings up their ammunition. Very unfortunate; for it will take us a little longer to beat these people.

In Billets.
December 22nd, 1914.

Your cake duly arrived. As, however, Major Baker also received one, we decided to eat his first, so mine is safely in its box, having escaped manifold dangers! Really one does have a complicated life of it at the front! To-day all my work was before me ready to do, when we received a frightened order to fall in at once, and did so. We were three hours at that game, and have not left the billets since. Various sorts of rumours reached us, the two most probable ones being that there were 6,000 Germans drawn up about two miles behind their lines, and the other that there was a fierce fight proceeding to the right of us. What those fights result in is the loss of anything up to 350 men and 14 or 15 officers, and we probably inflict twice that damage on the enemy. Well, this afternoon we have been covered with six-inch shells. Fortunately none have hit the house; but it is a constant strain. Yesterday we left our ruin and went back to these billets in the dark. We had to form up at certain cross roads, as a fight was raging, and I was afraid of spent bullets; I moved my men, who were waiting, under a house. No doubt they thought me rather a "funk," but appreciated my forethought when a few moments later two companies of another regiment were caught in the fire; one man had his head grazed, and another was hit through the back, narrowly missing his heart. Luckily, my doctor was with me, so that I was able to look after both of them at once. I saw in *The Times* that Austria had already been sounding Russia as to peace terms, but that she considered the terms proposed by Russia too hard. Of course she must make her choice, but she forgets that Hungary has nothing to lose by Russia's proposals and everything to gain, not only Peace. Russia's suggestion that Austria should make all her states, including Bohemia, into Federal States—viz., give them Home Rule—is exactly what Hungary wants, for she will then be head state of the Empire; not number two, as she is at present. Nothing would please her more than to see Austria broken up into a number of little States and Hungary ruling the roost. Well, these are my political remarks! It is a great blessing getting out of rifle fire, even for a minute. The constant strike of the bullets whirling round, or its scream as it ricochets over one's head, is very trying. I suppose there never has been a war in which one has required such staying power, excepting perhaps the Crimean expedition. It is late, so I must wish you good-bye.

Please send me more envelopes and writing paper.

In Trenches.
Christmas Eve, 1914.

I did not write to you yesterday, being extra busy. In the morning I had gone over on regimental business to see the Divisional Staff, and then on to inspect my transport, some miles back, out of shell fire. The unfortunate men are not so lucky as the horses, you see! Well, then I returned to luncheon with my General. Major B—— was with me, and we met there some officers of the Naval Brigade who defended Antwerp—or, rather, did not arrive in time to do so. Afterwards I hurried to my billet and hastily packed up all my kit, and marched the regiment down to the trenches. We had a new place to go to, somewhere nearer to the danger point of the line, I fancy. Well, one or two bullets came a bit too close as we were marching, and I was very thankful to get under cover. I am now in the ruins of a house. A shell had penetrated through it, but we stuffed up the hole with a bag of straw. The shattered windows are covered with boards in front; then we piled up bricks and nailed other boards behind. Between us and the enemy is a burnt-out house, which rings with the smack of the enemy's bullets as they hurtle against the wall or against the tiles. Opposite that, again, are our trenches, 400 yards away, and practically 400 yards from us also is the enemy's trench, as the line takes a bend there. I lie at nights ready armed, for one never knows what a minute may bring forth! I have told my people not to fire on Christmas Day if the enemy does not do so, but to trust him—*not at all!* So here I am spending Christmas Eve in the trenches—like my father did exactly 60 years ago in the Crimea.[9] Only I think I am a good bit more comfortable than he was at that time. I used to be up at cockcrow when a small child on Christmas Day, to see what Santa Claus had brought me, and I shall be up early enough to-morrow in all conscience too, but for a different reason—standing to arms—so that I shall not get my throat cut. The news of troubles in Berlin looks encouraging. However, one must not build too much on that, but I have great hopes of Hungary and Austria coming out of the war. To-day I have been round my new trenches; only half of them are new, though, and, as usual, are swimming in liquid mud. One of the men there had to be carried away with his eye knocked out by a bullet which had come through the parapet. Again my casualties for killed and wounded you can find by multiplying the number of your uncle's house in Dublin by three, and then subtracting ten from the total. [This number would be 98.]

I suppose our sick are more than twice that amount. Best of love to you for Christmas. Whilst you are in church I shall be in the trenches, but both doing our rightful duty, I trust.

Yours ever,
G.B.L.

As to school for Hal, you have done quite rightly. Mrs. Napier has a pet school for boys, kept by a cousin of hers, I fancy, that ought to be a fairly useful one.

G.B.L.

"CHRISTMAS IN THE CRIMEA.

"How it was Celebrated near Balaclava in 1854.
"By Lieut.-General Laurie, C.B., M.P.

"In some of his Christmas annuals Charles Dickens delighted to portray the misanthropic grumbler who hated to see others enjoy themselves, and always laid himself out to be especially miserable at Christmas time, exaggerating the effects of the season by assuming a frozen aspect, and like an iceberg, chilling all around him; yet as the same iceberg when swept into the Gulf Stream finds the surrounding air and water by which it is enveloped will not admit its retaining its frigid isolation, it gradually melts and mixes with the warmer current, so Dickens brought his surly and crabbed man in contact with those who had set themselves to see everything under its brightest aspect, and under these softening influences he gradually thaws out and becomes the merriest amongst the merry, carried away by the joyous influences that are associated with the keeping of Christmas. And in all English-speaking countries, and especially in our old home, England, it is looked upon as a season to be given up entirely to pleasure in the present and bright hopes for the future. Memory takes me back to a Christmas which hardly came up to the ideal, and the contrast of then and now, of trials and miseries endured then, as compared with present comforts, may make us more satisfied with, and thankful for what we now enjoy. Twenty-nine years ago England had contributed as her share of the Crimean invading force over 35,000 men, of whom a scanty 8,000 were on Christmas Day, 1854, available for duty; many of the remainder had helped to fill the huge trenches hastily dug for graves on the fields of Alma and Inkerman, or slept below the innumerable little mounds which surrounded our camp hospitals, and inside the canvas walls of these the number of sick exceeded the total of those who still stood in the ranks, although none were received into hospital as long as they were able to carry themselves and their rifles. During the greater part of December we had been reduced to half rations, and sometimes to no meat at all; half a pound of biscuit; one blanket, and threadbare suit of uniform contributed but small support and protection to meet a climate not unlike that of Nova Scotia. And we were entirely without fuel, other than the roots of small alder bushes, which were grubbed up with pickaxes carried off from the trenches, and sometimes the pickaxe handles were used to warm a canteen of water for tea. But soon these became so scarce that we were without a single fire in the camp of my regiment for three days. In spite of all, however, Christmas was at hand, and we all set ourselves to be jolly. Even the celebrated Mark Tapley would have considered the circumstances were fairly creditable. The authorities also considered it incumbent on them to make an extra effort, and it was announced with great pride that the commissariat had secured some live cattle in honour of the season, and we were to receive an issue of fresh meat. But this was the extent of their ambition, and their pride met with a fall, for, after waiting till after three o'clock, our pioneers, who drew the rations, returned with the melancholy intelligence that there was nothing for us that day. 'The Zouaves,' so said the commissariat officers, 'had stolen the bullocks.' It is often mentioned as one of the advantages of live cattle as food for an army that they require no transport, but carry themselves. But we learnt that there is another side to this quality—they sometimes carry themselves away, as they did on this occasion. Whether our gallant allies really ate our dinner as well as their own that Christmas Day I know not, but African warfare had taught them to take care of No. 1, and they formed a convenient and not unlikely peg on which to hang the deficiency; and deficiency there was, for our supply department, relying upon their fresh meat, had not brought up any salt meat from Balaclava, and we were left with only our ration biscuit for our Christmas dinner. Just as we received this pleasant intelligence the orderly sergeant handed me the order book warning me I was for guard duty in the trenches that night. Our regiment, which had gone out from Edinburgh in the spring over 1,000 strong, and had received a reinforcement of nearly 100 men, was at this time reduced to 68 men available for duty. So but one captain and one lieutenant (myself) were detailed to take charge of this poor remnant of what had been, three months before, a magnificent battalion. Captain Patrick Robertson, well known to Haligonians as Colonel Robertson-Ross, Adjutant-General of Canadian Militia, was to be my companion. A new colonel had just been sent to us from a West Indian regiment, who took as much interest in his new command as if he had served all his life with us, and employed his chargers and his grooms to transport any possible comforts for his men. Six months afterwards he was struck down when directing the fire of his men on the Russian gunners to keep down their fire and cover our attack on the Redan. By chance he heard us warned for guard, and at once went to his tent and returned with a ham knuckle. 'It is all I have,' he said, 'but those going on duty must have the first chance of some food on Christmas Day. Sit down on your rug and make the best of it.' He was in earnest, so we ate up his dinner and polished the ham bone; but I had determined to keep Christmas as an Englishman should with a real plum pudding. I had collected the ingredients in the course of a couple of trips among the Maltese and Greek settlers at

Balaclava and from the stewards of some of the transports; a few raisins, a little sugar, some butter (so called by courtesy); and of course my ration rum came into play. I could not get any flour, so purchased some biscuit at Balaclava. It was mouldy and full of weevils, and had been condemned as ship's stores and sold to some camp followers, but to us at half a crown a pound it was a treasure. I pounded a quantity of this as fine as possible, and mixed the material in my tin shako case, which did duty as bucket, etc., and tied them up in one of my two towels, and, having secured a tent bag full of freshly dug alder roots, the pudding was put on to boil. As we were going on guard, dinner was early, perhaps too early for the pudding. We had no holly, and could not spare spirits enough to make a blaze, but my servant brought in the pudding quite as triumphantly as if we had been in baronial mansion in old England. It was reserved for me to open the towel, which I did with no little pride at having the only plum pudding in camp. I had buttered the towel so that it should not stick to it; it did not, but it did not stick together either. It would not stand up, but fell apart like very stiff porridge. I believe it wasn't bad to eat, but it wasn't exactly what we understand to be plum pudding. My vanity was cruelly mortified after all my efforts to excel. I have never attempted to make another plum pudding. The Russians were considerate that night. They gave us very little annoyance, and Robertson and I walked up and down in rear of the trenches where our weary and worn-out men were lying quiet, getting a welcome rest in a half-wet, half-frozen ditch. We talked of home and how we had spent other Christmases, but I do not think we either expressed or held any other thought for the future than when we should bring our discomforts to an end and wind up the siege by a determined attack on Sebastopol. Little we expected that after long separation our paths would again come together in America, serving the Canadian Government in the organization of its militia. And amongst the sad memories which intertwine with the pleasures of this present Christmas is that of my poor comrade, a brilliant out-post officer and a gallant man, who, after facing every form of danger as a soldier should, died a few months since from violent seasickness, brought on in crossing the English Channel. Memory conjures up the past at this season. Friends who have left us are present in spirit. We associate the past with the present more at Christmas than at any other time of year. It colours our thoughts and influences our acts unknown to us, and brings out kindly feelings and hope, as much in 1883 as my reminiscences show it did in 1854."

GENERAL LAURIE AND HIS THREE SONS IN 1901.

In Trenches,
Christmas Day, 1914.

Here we are, on Christmas Day! We have had a curious time of it. Last night, about eleven o'clock, the enemy (100 yards only from us) put lanterns up on the parapet and called out: "Do not shoot after twelve o'clock, and we will not do so either." One of our men ventured across; he was not fired upon, and was given a cigar and told to go back. A German officer came out next, and asked for two days' truce from firing, but we said, "Only one day." Then we saw both sides, English and German, begin to swarm out to meet each other; we thought it wiser to keep our men in, because we did not trust the Germans, so I rang up the General to tell him this. We had to station sentries on the trenches to keep the men back; they were so eager to talk to the Germans. Then I offered to go across myself and learn what I could, and finally the German General asked me to send one of our officers over to them. This I did, and gave the latter as an ostensible reason the *Daily Telegraph* of December 22nd, which I had got hold of, and which contained a very fair account of the troubles in Austria-Hungary and Berlin. He went out with this paper, met some German officers, and discovered a certain amount. They were very anxious to know if the Canadian Division had arrived, whether our trenches were very muddy, and told him that our rifle fire was good. We said that our rifle fire in general was our weak point, etc., etc. So now this is the queer position of affairs: we fire a pistol shot off at 12 midnight to-night by arrangement, and they reply with some shots over our heads, after which things continue to hum as before. You have no idea how pleasant everything seems with no rifle bullets or shells flying about. I need hardly tell you that we have kept our men ready in the trenches all the same, as we do not trust our friends further than we can see them. As to other matters. (1) The pheasants and the partridges arrived in time, and we lunched off them sumptuously to-day; many thanks. (2) The chocolate arrived, and was distributed this afternoon to the men. (3) I enclose three Christmas cards. They are very hard to get, and you had better keep them as mementoes of this war. I am sending one to my Mother. (4) Only 500 lbs. of plum pudding arrived for our men this afternoon. If more does not turn up to-morrow, I will write to the A.D.C. of General Rawlinson to find out what has happened to the remainder. Whilst we are peaceable, the guns are booming out now and then some miles away on our left and right where the French are fighting. I suppose we all thought from the Germans' behaviour that they had something up their sleeves and are looking out for squalls. They said that their army was in Moscow, and that the Russians were beaten, and, moreover, that the war would be over in two, or at most three weeks, so we are expecting a push....

Still in Trenches.
December 26th, 1914.

Your letters came last night. Many thanks for sending mincepies, which have not yet appeared, but which will have justice done to them when they do turn up. As to your large bales of clothing, I believe they have arrived. I must say "believe" because my duties are so many that I have had to tell off one of my officers to look after these affairs; he then reports their arrival to me, bringing in the card enclosed in the bundle, etc. Sometimes they do not all come in one body, but perhaps one bundle to-day and another two days later. I think, however, that practically the whole five have now arrived. There are so many things that we are actually storing, some in a hired building behind the lines, for the men can neither wear nor carry them. I hear that poor Mr. Aitchison has lost his son; he was in the fourth King's Own, my father's as well as my brother H.'s old corps. The Kaiser has come to this part of the world, it is said, so I expect we shall hear of some strong fighting soon. Our "friends" fired one shot at 12 midnight as arranged, but have been quiet ever since. Perhaps they are tired of the war, and want to get home. I expect you are very busy about Christmas things. Do not overtire yourself. How very kind of my Mother to send £25 to our Funds! I must write and thank her. In the meantime, we do not really require anything; will let you know when we do. I am told that all regiments are much the same. Matches are an exception, and are always welcome, but they must be *safety* ones to go through the post. Frost this morning, though nothing very cold as yet; still the sheepskin will probably be most useful if I can wear and carry it, but it has its difficulties. Thank the children for their cards, please....

In Billets.
December 27th, 1914.

Our strange sort of armistice continued throughout yesterday. The Germans told us they were all Landwehr men, and therefore not obliged to fight outside Germany except as volunteers, and that they did not intend to fight at present. Sure enough, though we shelled them and fired at them with rifles, they paid not the slightest attention. Whilst the shelling was on, they dodged down in their trenches, and popped up again when it was over. We hit one with a rifle, but as they would not reply, we felt rather mean and fired over their heads. The relieving regiment [Lincolnshire], of which Mr. Brown of South Collingham is a member, said they would not go on like this. Curiously enough, they have done so. Leaving our trenches, we marched away gaily, getting in here about eight o'clock, or a little later. Had something to eat; then I crawled between my blankets, having, as usual, been up just before 5 o'clock the previous night. At 10.30 p.m. we were waked by a message: "The Germans are attacking at midnight. A deserter has just come in to say so." Out we turned immediately, and marched in very cold weather to a certain point. There we halted; our guns had already opened a dreadful fire on the ground where the enemy must have been assembling his assaulting columns. Apparently this took the heart out of him, for the attack did not come off. I very much thought that this night would probably be my last. However, about 2.30 a.m. we decided to put the men into any ruins near us, and after stopping for some time in a blacksmith's shop seated on a sheaf of straw, I managed to get into a room with a concrete floor, and went to sleep there, having borrowed a sort of thin wrap from a Frenchman and put a sack over my feet to keep them from freezing. About 6.15 a.m. the Frenchman gave us some warm milk, and I was able to give him in return some of your excellent chocolate, whilst we also partook of it too. By 8 o'clock we were back in our billets. I had luncheon with my own General (Brigadier-General Lowry Cole). I hear that the enemy are walking about again on their parapets—refusing to fight. Church this morning in the unruined chapel of a small convent which has escaped the attention of the Huns! Apparently the people do not mind our using it. The central light of the east window represents a figure of the Blessed Virgin Mary, but a lot of my Presbyterians come all the same....

Later on 27.12.14.

I am still in my hole in the earth. Very horrid. Have not washed nor shaved for two days, and am covered with mud from head to foot in thick layers. If I raise my head to stand up straight, a bullet skips about my ears. I went round my trenches last night from 7 p.m. till 12.5 a.m. Such a walk! For some four hours I was travelling as hard as I could in the mud, slipping down in filthy ditches, entering in narrow cuttings in the earth made to protect one from sniping, and called concentration trenches. Still, we got round and held the line afterwards, despite the miseries of the situation. Sometimes I had to crawl on hands and knees through tiny places. I fancy that a pig is a happier creature than I am at present! When I arrived home at my particular burrow, I found a bundle of correspondence waiting for me to be answered to the Brigadier, so that had to be done in my ruin. Was up at 4.30 a.m. to try to see about the men's food and teas for the coming day, and filling of water-bottles, all of which has to be accomplished in the dark. I have had a very trying time working night and day lately. No sleep the day before, and none excepting three hours last night. This makes 72 hours up to 5 o'clock to-day, with only three hours' rest. As I sit here I can hear the shells booming near us, and very heavy fighting on the left, whilst a solitary sniper keeps pouring bullets over my head, hitting all round the houses some four hundred yards behind me. I ask no questions, but think that we cannot possibly be relieved under four more days, and that we shall be very, very dirty at the end!

In Billets.
December 28th, 1914.

Two private plum puddings arrived last night; many thanks. I turned in at 8.30 p.m., and slept peacefully and heavily till 7.30 a.m., and would have slept longer, only an orderly from the Brigade Office woke me with his gentle tread on carpetless boards! I had one other interval during the night listening to our guns all blazing away together for quite a long time. Presumably they are trying to catch the Germans forming up somewhere for an attack. You ought to be near a six-inch shell when it bursts to hear the sort of "scruntling" wrench that it gives as it breaks up the tough outer steel. To-day I have been arranging to have my men and their clothes washed, for such things have to go on in war as well as in peace time, only I am obliged to have the clothes fumigated as well now. My own hair has not been cut since I left Winchester, but I will try to see to that this afternoon! The weather has broken from frost into a heavy drizzle, which ought to make the trenches a sight, with the mud that is in them already, when we go back. I have written to my Mother thanking her for her generous gift to the Regiment. I fear she is alarmed at my being out here.... I am going for a walk this afternoon to try to get some life into my toes; they have been quite dead since we went into the trenches for the first time. Probably they are really all right, though I cannot feel anything as yet in them. Gen. Davis tells me that we are shooting away at the enemy to-day, but still they will not fight. Our last hostess was the daughter of a gamekeeper; that was where we had some milk yesterday morning. She said that her father escaped the Germans by jumping on a horse and riding 20 miles. I think I could have walked that distance easily for the same reason. Col. Napier told me that his boy Charlie was captured by the Germans at school at Hanover, "which," he added, "doesn't make me love my enemies any more."...

In Billets.
December 29th, 1914.

We are off to-night for the trenches again. I hear that the Germans spent their time shelling our particular ones. It is to be hoped that they have used up their ammunition for the present, as I believe they are rather short. Such a night as it was; blowing a raging gale; but one gets very selfish, and we only remarked: "What an awful night in the trenches! Please God the Germans do not attack! Thank God we are not in them to-night!" and that was all. I wonder how long this war will go on. It never seems to come to an end, does it? I walked yesterday afternoon to a small town beyond shell fire and had my hair cut at last. I also had tea with a Capt. Sherlock, whose wife, I think, was a friend of yours, one of Sir Francis Cruise's daughters, "Gussie." I heard from Major Alston, of the 2nd Bat., how Capt. Whelan was killed. He showed great courage, and stood up on a parapet to demonstrate to his men where he wanted some digging done, only 250 yds. from the Germans. Of course he was seen at once, and was hit in the lungs. Major A—— also said that he was commanding that Battalion, and it was full of strange officers, but I expect they are doing all right. I fancy our German friends are finding the war longer than they thought. A curious coincidence is that we are opposed to the 25th German Infantry Brigade, that, of course, being our own number. So far we have not received Princess Mary's boxes. We shall get them in time, and I shall let you know later on about the plum puddings when I hear from the A.D.C. I did not get a letter from you last night, no doubt owing to Christmas Day and delayed posts....

In Trenches.
December 30th, 1914.

Just returned to my ruin from my trenches. They are up nearly to the waist in water, with little islands here and there for the men. I am absolutely trembling with cold, though I have changed my garments. Whilst I was there poor Capt. Miles, attached to me, was shot through the head. Being close by, I waded to him, but it was hopeless from the first. Such a place to die in!—but Heaven will be Heaven after that. His poor wife, too. I must write to her. He was a very nice man. I had plenty of morphia given to him, and he is now dying without any pain quite peacefully. Coming away from him, the German snipers spotted me, and twice I was covered with mud from their bullets; a near shave! It is a good thing to be able to look forward to Heaven as a home. I only wish I could realize it even more than I do. I will write you again as soon as we get into billets when I can find my valise. I think at Carlton you are fairly safe from air raids....

P.S.—Mincepies tried to-day are excellent. I have heard from Capt. Boscawen about the plum pudding. It seems that a portion had to go to other regiments of the Brigade, but I should like you to send over some more for my Regiment only as soon as you can conveniently order it. Princess Mary's present has arrived, and I have sent it across to you for safe custody. The keeper might like the pipe and tobacco. I am sure you will appreciate the brass box as a memento, for we have both won it very hardly.... I have just been to see poor Capt. Miles carried out on a stretcher dead. I wonder how much of this war and the deaths caused by it will rest on the Kaiser's shoulders. I must now write a further letter to go to his wife. He was a talented man, and used to write for papers. When the war broke out he was running a cinematograph film-collecting expedition in German East Africa, and just managed to get away. Poor fellow!

G.B.L. 30.12.14.

LETTERS OF JANUARY, 1915.

In Billets.
January 2nd, 1915.

My dear F——

I am not asking you to do anything to-day for me, as I hope to come in person, leaving here on Monday morning. The hour of my arrival at Carlton depends on whether I can get through quickly or not, and whether the Kaiser tries to sink the Boulogne to Folkestone boat. Knowing his peculiarities, I think he would probably wait until he found an emigrant ship well laden with women and children. What brutes the Germans have proved themselves! After heavy rain, the day has turned out bright and cold. The ditches are nearly full of water, which means that all communication trenches will be worse than ever, and Heaven knows they are bad enough already! Yes, I sent some of my private affairs to Carlton to await my return after this war, when I can attend to them, if I really do come back.... There are moments I wonder if anyone will!... *The Times* of December 28th gave the names of 45 officers killed and 66 wounded between December 21st and 24th. We were fighting fairly hard all the while, but still, if we are as one to nine of the French, this shows that our combined losses would be roughly 1,100 officers for four days, before you come to the men. How matters stand with the Germans can only be conjectured. We learnt from a prisoner the other day that we had inflicted such terrible losses that they had been obliged to change their hour of relieving trenches. As a matter of fact, it had not occurred to us that we had given them any losses at all to speak of at those particular times. Anyhow, if Germany is losing as it is said she is in proportion of three to one of our men, the war cannot continue indefinitely. I hear the fight on my right and on my left at Ypres and La Bassée, both places being hard fought for by the opposing sides, and the row is sometimes deafening. As to your inquiries about Major Abadie, there is nothing to be said. If alive, he ought to have been heard of before now. Probably the poor fellow is dead, and was buried by the Germans or by the Belgian peasants, and no one will ever know what has become of him. A lot of Christmas cards have been sent to me ... but of course I cannot carry them about ... I am afraid mine is very much a soldier's faith. It seems to me one's duty is placed in front of one by Providence, and that if one carries it out faithfully and honestly, whate'er befalls, it is well, ... and this, I am sure, is the creed of all good soldiers. The shelling is making the house shake, but nothing very serious, I think, at present.

Yours....
G——.

In Billets.
January 3rd, 1915.

Just across the farmyard under my windows is the barn where my Catholic men are having High Mass, and where in half an hour, if alive, we shall have our service too. There was a good precedent for stables, I believe, 1915 years ago, so we do not view it as incongruous, but I understand that High Mass is unusual, and no doubt a great honour to the Regiment. I hear that our leave does not come off till January 6th. That puts me into the trenches to-morrow night again, for a short time. Last night, about 10.30 o'clock, I was snuggled in my blankets, not very well, for ice-cold water has a way of making you feel it after you are forty-four! However, I was awakened by a tremendous bombardment, all our guns going around us. It broke out twice again: I knew then what it was by putting two and two together. We had found out from a prisoner that the Germans were changing their trench troops about that time, and if we managed to catch them, we must have done them much harm. Rode over to inspect my transport yesterday. Incidentally, Major Baker and I bought 1-½ doz. eggs at four for a franc. Famine price, of course, but I have only seen two since I came over here! As to the discomfort of this work, it is not very pleasant, but I do not trouble greatly about it. As an unmarried man, I should not mind the danger either very much, having had a certain amount of experience in Egypt and South Africa, but as a married man, I hate it, because I think it would probably make a great difference to our young people when they grow up if I get killed. Sybil R—— wrote to me yesterday. You know I am her trustee. As to matches, etc., for the troops, keep all waiting now till I get over, and then it will be easy to help you about these things. Well, I must stop to go to church, and there is a good deal also for me to see to afterwards....

January 4th, 1915.

No letter from you last night. So far, no further news of my leave either, but I believe it is due on January 6th all right. Slight rheumatism, that is only to be expected. It has been raining hard, and we are off to the trenches to-night, and I should think they will be worth seeing. It is said that the ground our trenches now occupy will soon be turned into a lake, and we shall have to go boating there. I warned the General the other day in fun that he would require boats ere long to bring up our rations, and it is really coming true! Such a cold, bleak day as it is! I am going over to the Cashier to try to get some money to bring me home; this is the only way one has of obtaining funds in this part of the world. Sad thing about that man-of-war being sunk. What beasts the Germans are with their mines, to be sure! Up to now the lambskin coat has not yet appeared, but I received a note saying that it was sent off on December 30th, so it ought to turn up some time or other, and then one can see. I suppose, if I get through this war, it would always come in as a lining for a motoring coat. Well, I must close this epistle and dash off, as I have to see to many other things before luncheon. We march to the trenches this afternoon.

G.B.L.

I shall telegraph from Folkestone, if I can; probably I shall come by the 8.30 p.m. train on the 6th, but I am only guessing. It may be January 7th.

[*Note.*—An interval occurs from the date of this letter, when Colonel Laurie obtained ten days' leave and returned to England.]

IN TRENCHES AGAIN.
January 13th, 1915.

My dear F——

After leaving C.-on-T. I met Mrs. Foley in London, and gave her a note to post to you. As you know, I spent the night at 24, Harrington Gardens. I was up at 6 a.m., and Aunt M—— (Mrs. Cowell) had a lovely breakfast for me. I was away by 7.30, catching my train all right at Victoria. It was run in two parts. We had a rough crossing to Boulogne, but I was not ill. We reached railhead at 8 p.m., and I then mounted my horse and rode along the quiet country road in the dark. The others travelled in wagons; I preferred riding to driving in farm-carts. On arriving at my transport lines, I changed and came on here, getting in about 12.30 a.m. My people had left their house, having had a shell in the room we lived in, which had blown it even more to bits than before. I went to our new abode, and then on to the trenches to see how everything was doing, and got wet half way to the knees in the driest parts; but I am glad to say they are steadily improving things for us Regimental officers. I was in bed between 2 and 3 a.m., rose again at 3.30, and finally, of course, just about 5 a.m. for good. My feet were rather numbed after the cold water, as we had to break the ice at every step. This morning the Frenchwoman visited us. Each time she comes we are shelled, and Major Baker is sure that she is a spy. To-day was no exception; we were well slated, and two shrapnel hit the roof. Fortunately the firing has now stopped. These Germans are malicious brutes, and would be glad to do one an injury. Mincepies arrived the worse for travelling, though much appreciated all the same. I want to find out more about your suggestion for khaki flannel shirts. So far, everyone thinks they would be most useful, but I must ask all the others. I believe they would be gladly accepted, as the matches were this morning, with joy. It is nice to think I managed to get over to see you.... Heard yesterday that the authorities are still hopeful as to Germany running short of ammunition, but, of course, the more we can get out of her the better. Some big shells are falling near us now, whether theirs or ours I have not ascertained....

In Billets.
January 14th, 1915.

So far, of course, no letter from England, though one may arrive to-night. I beat the post by a little, you see! I heard from Lord Grenfell yesterday on some business matters. He tells me that the Russians were in a critical state three weeks ago with their ammunition used up. I imagine, as he says, that they have now got it, and their reinforcements, etc., are quite right again. I also heard from Sir Charles Burnett, our Colonel. Enclosed is Mrs. Miles's letter, a most broken-hearted one. I am writing to her, poor lady, again to assure her that her husband's sword will be sent home. We came peacefully out of the trenches yesterday, though Major Baker, who marches before me, had plenty of bullets round him. To-day I have been examining my new draft of men, quite a useful lot, and in the afternoon rode over to inspect my transport. You see I have got the pad you sent me, and am using it at once. About H—— I approve of his going to Stanmore Park in a year's time. He will then be 9-½.

G.B.L.

P.S.—The sheepskin has at last arrived. Thank you for your kind present, but I am almost afraid that it will not work. It is much too bulky! Even Major B—— looked queerly at it! By the way, the cake also came; it was beautifully fresh. We do enjoy these things. Many thanks for both. The sheepskin is very short for me, and closely cropped, and looks like a worn-out mat!!

In Billets.
January 15th, 1915.

Two letters arrived from you to-night, enclosing also a nice one from Mr. Argles, etc., etc., and I will write to him about January 20th, if I get out of the trenches safely this time! I wonder what the change of Austria's Foreign Minister means. Everything in the way of change can, I think, only be to the good of England, as Hungary has always been friendly to us. Our General inspected us this morning at 11 a.m. My first parade was at 5.45 a.m., and I had another at mid-day, and yet another look round later in the evening after dark. I also went for a hack to examine a road behind our position. So all this passes the time. *Re* the khaki flannel. What the officers think is as follows: They would like shirts very much, but as everybody bought new ones when they were home in October, they are not required at present, though those they now have will very soon be worn out, and then they would be grateful for others, and it would save them trouble. So you could have the shirts made up by the woman you speak of, giving her good brown bone buttons. At least ten of them could be a copy of my flannel ones, with single button cuffs instead of the double kind which have "holes for links." There are several officers in the Battalion who take my size in shirts, and the remainder could be made a bit smaller. Most people are rather ill after the trench warfare of the last two days. I had a head, too, nothing worse. It has been wonderfully mild here. I am keeping my lambskin coat after all. I think one could use it to sleep in on cold nights, or to do work in too, but I hope I shall not want it, as half the winter is over. Good-bye.

Yours....
G———.

In Billets.
January 16th, 1915.

Am off in a moment on duty, winding up with luncheon at my General's before I go to the trenches. Following out that note from the Saddler's Co. I have written to ask for some comforts for my men. Not clothes, but what do you think? Coffee and milk in tins. Then this morning I have been practising bomb-throwers. This Christian device is made of a jam-tin or crock filled with gun-cotton and nails, and has a fuse attached to it. The fuse is lighted and thrown by hand into the enemy's trench, where it explodes and does much execution. Cheerful, is it not? Another plan of mine was rather unpleasant. I told you that I pumped the water out of our trenches into the German ones, and that they replied, and then dam-building began. Finally, we burst their dam, and some men working on it fled. Our people were about to fire, seeing them running, when an old soldier called out: "Do not shoot, for they cannot run far in that mud." The poor things finally stopped, panting, and they had to be shot down as they stood. Such is war. Very hideous, and I loathe it, but what will you? I am sure fighting is the thing I hate of all others, but I object more to these Huns coming over to England and knocking our women and children about.

In Trenches.
January 17th, 1915.

Here I am back again in my trenches. During the three days we did "support" the enemy blew up several houses in this road with shells. Now they are being shelled by our guns, and I am afraid the scamps will fire on us again when the gunners go to dinner. We got in quite peacefully last night, and after something to eat, politely called "dinner," I flew off to see and direct my trench working parties. Starting about 8.30 o'clock, I arrived home between 1 and 2 a.m. Was up again at 5.30 on parade. At 7.30 the General came out. I had a working party of 50 Royal Artillery men as well as my own. We dug away hard whilst the Germans sent occasional bullets amongst us and threw rockets to try to show us up: we lay down then to prevent having machine guns turned on us. But now that we are making the dry parapets I advocated, things are much better in every way, and everyone is more cheery. In building these parapets, the materials have to be carried across drains and even disused trenches, the ground in some places being seamed with old diggings. Last night I saw two men fall into these ditches in the dark, and we had to fish them out. One fell about six feet into about four feet of water. The whole thing was most weird, with the rockets flying and bullets going, and working parties shovelling for dear life in the darkness. We all tumbled about into shell-holes or ditches in turn, where the water is very cold. I suppose the utter hopelessness of it all prevents one getting ill. The mails are late, so I have not received your letter to-night. This morning, when walking with the General, we came upon a Frenchman, woman, and boy in the fire zone 600 yds. from the German trenches wheeling two large wheelbarrows full of household goods which they had removed from some local houses to take back to another ruin where they were living, out of shell fire. Of course the stuff was theirs, but these poor things always forget that, besides their own safety, they bring fire on the houses near them, so we had to send them roughly away; but I did feel so sorry, and in the end persuaded the General to promise them a pass for to-night so as to get the wheelbarrows away. Practice makes perfect, for I spoke to them more or less in fluent French! I never told you what a comfort the watch you gave me has been. It keeps excellent time, and is most reliable. I must try and get some sleep to-day, as I foresee another busy night, and my feet are so cold, the result, I suppose, of two long tramps in ice-cold water. May the war soon cease!

P.S.—Heavy firing, Ypres way.

In Trenches.
January 18th, 1915.

Here we are in a snowstorm! I received your note of 14th last night. Not bad, when it has to get to London, leave our base, and come part of the way to the trenches upon foot for safety. I really sent the account of our Christmas luncheon to you. It was an R.A. captain who lunched with us, and afterwards wrote to his people about it. They published the letter, and I found it in *The Times* I got from you, and sent it forward through Major Baker via Mrs. Baker. There is not much news. We are still alive.... My ruin looks out directly towards the Germans (I hear a bullet hitting it now). As the place where the window was is quite open, I have had it filled up with bags of earth piled one above the other, and I sleep with my head under these and hope for the best. Last night we had two adventures. Our "friends" pitched a high-explosive shell after dark with such a true aim that the pieces flew all about our ruin, in and out of the rooms. They followed this with three more, but they were farther off. The second thing was that my Sergeant-Major, Master Cook, and Sergeant-Bugler, all trembling with cold, poor dears! shut themselves up last night with a charcoal fire, and we found them about four o'clock insensible from the fumes, and had a certain amount of difficulty in bringing them round. Here in war time these people do different things. For instance, the Master Cook has a party of bomb-throwers formed from among the cooks. The Sergeant-Major, instead of drilling the Battalion, arrives up with 8 mules and three ammunition carts, whilst the Sergeant-Bugler, instead of discoursing unsweet music on a bugle, converts his buglers into a corps of messengers to bring me letters or to take them out to my companies.

I was round again last night, not much shot at personally, though chance bullets flew overhead in an embarrassing way, hitting the ground in various places. Capt. Tee had a couple of narrow escapes yesterday while he was out with us. I was inspecting our dressing station arranging about our little cemetery with the doctor and Capt. Wright, when a bullet cut the grass beside us in a most uncalled for manner. So it goes on, and so I hope the war will shortly wind up. I expect things are not very cosy in Germany either!...

In Trenches.
January 19th, 1915.

Two letters from you last night up to January 16th. Poor little Blanche, having her teeth out! They do hurt! Had more Christmas cards sent on from Aden. A fairly quiet day yesterday, though there is always fighting Ypres way, and we hear it plainly. This morning I was out at four a.m. with the Brigade Major, and took up the running afterwards with the General about 8 o'clock. I assured him that a certain trench was not the place for him, but he said he had a special wish to visit it, so with his usual dauntless courage off we went. Next minute a bullet hit the ground right between us. After that he thought it wise to retire, and we marched away homeward. My feet were practically frozen with the cold water, and I can't say I was sorry to leave. The authorities, however, are issuing some stuff which is supposed to keep the feet warm, so I propose getting hold of some to sample the next time I come to the trenches, and shall tell you of the results. I must write a letter to Mr. Aitchison to-morrow when I arrive in billets and get hold of some notepaper. It looks to me very dull, like rain or snow. I expect more plum puddings and pheasants are waiting for me when I get out. Thank you for them in anticipation. I fancy that Germany has had an awful eye-opener. In her big war with France in July, 1870, which she has lived on for the last forty-five years, the fighting was over in January, 1871. Now it is just beginning for her. Still, I cannot help thinking that peace is in sight somewhere soon.

Yours....
G.B.L.

We go into reserve to-night for 3 days, and need not get up at 5 a.m. Great joy!

In Billets.
January 20th, 1915.

We marched out of the trenches successfully last night, getting in here about nine o'clock. Then I had to see to my company commanders and a lot of other work too, for a regiment will not run itself properly unless someone looks after it. I was rather amused at a case I had this morning of an N.C.O. charged with letting his rifle become dirty. He admitted the offence, but stated that whilst he was watching everyone out of the trenches, he heard cries for help, and found a small rifleman stuck in a ditch up to his shoulders, and that he was carrying, besides his rifle, a pick and shovel; so the N.C.O. went to his aid and got engulfed too. Hence his trouble about his rifle. The enemy, to prevent our forgetting him, is throwing big shells into the place we are billeted in. As he knows, probably, that the women and children have returned here, he expects with luck to make a big bag of such non-combatants. It was luxury last night getting into bed again without boots, even if one had no other night attire! You will be pleased to hear that your tobacco arrived this morning. The people who sent it were not very bright, for, despite the fact that my address was plainly painted on every box, they had stupidly nailed on other cards marked from Griffith, Solicitor, S. Wales, and addressed to the S. Wales Borderers or 24th Regiment. This was done to at least half of the cases. Apparently they had stuck them on the wrong boxes. Whether this accounts for the delay I cannot say. Anyhow, each box had 15 lbs. of tobacco, and I think there were 16 boxes. Well, then your last lot of plum pudding arrived, and has been issued to be eaten to-morrow. There were 65 tins containing four and a half lbs. each, so I think, my dear, that the men will be grateful to you. There was also a large bale of things like cigarettes and gloves from other associations, but nothing to touch your consignments. We had to turn out of our happy ruin twice yesterday afternoon whilst the enemy threw high-explosive shells our way, and just missed us. Fortunately his supply of ammunition is said to be running short, or he would do worse mischief. I had a very nice letter from my Mother and from Meta yesterday.... Your pheasants have come, also the ham, very well packed. Biscuits a little knocked about, but still edible; many thanks for them all. It is so misty and cold, a typical raw day in your own hunting district. Best of love, and hoping that the war will soon be over....

In Billets.
January 21st, 1915.

Got some of the French mud off my men yesterday, took the horse out to examine the neighbouring roads in case of a retreat, and dined with the General. He, poor man, finds the times very evil and the enemy very strong. I have written to my Mother to-day, telling her how I propose spending her present to me. By the way, I only got my trophies in time across to England. Four days ago an Army Order came out that nothing was allowed to be taken away, and that all such things found must be taken to the depots. Of course we must do so for the future, though I hope to be able to borrow a Prussian helmet with luck before I come home again. In the meantime, have the other stuff cleaned up and lacquered; it keeps rust off, and saves the servants much trouble. The A. and N. Stores can do this if you cannot get it well done in Newark.... Poor Mrs. Miles! She is dreadfully cut up. Capt. Allgood and Capt. Miles are now gone. I liked them both, but we shall meet again face to face some day.... I only wish that I could impress this more on one's daily thoughts and walk of life. Well, I do not mean to preach, but it comes in my lowland Scotch blood, I suppose!...

January 22nd, 1915.

Thanks for your note last night of January 19th. As you say, considering war time, this is quick. But at present it is a stationary war, and there is no reason why it should not be so. Once we get on the move, you will see that things will work badly, and we shall be short of food and of mails too. I was glad to get Aunt B——'s letter. Yesterday was an absolute drench. I rode, all the same, for exercise, and on the way back the enemy proceeded to shell the road; at the very extremity of their range, I fancy. It is curious how one takes the shelling nowadays. One becomes a fatalist! "If it hits me, it must hit me; I cannot escape, but I hope it will not" sort of thing. We return to the trenches this afternoon. Our General leaves to-night, but before then he has elected to inspect our billets in the afternoon, and to have a night alarm in the trenches early this evening. All the Colonels have therefore put their heads together to keep things as right as possible for him. Major Baker also goes on leave for about 10 days or so to-night, with various other officers who have well earned a rest. I see you had Zeppelins over you yesterday, or rather the day before; but I think that where you live you are as safe as anywhere in England. It shows what gentlemen these Germans are in the way they treat non-combatants.

To-day is a bright rather beautiful frosty day, and I am going to look at a large church in a village on a road when reconnoitring. I went to see another two days ago, and found only the tower and the walls standing; the Germans had burnt the rest.

P.S.—The billets we leave to-day are like a very tiny 9th-rate hotel, about as large as the house opposite the blacksmith's forge at Carlton, or a little larger, with another storey added on. Tiny rooms, and stoves in only two of them, which can be used as sitting-rooms. We found a small tub, to our great delight, and this allows us first to wash ourselves and then our things, so we are perfectly happy in it....

In Trenches.
January 23rd, 1915.

We arrived at our trenches all right last night, and, as I had expected, found them fairly under water. In parts it was like the ground round that pretty little cottage at Carlton, where Thompson lives when the Trent is in flood. I was crossing, gingerly trying not to get my feet wet, when a machine gun opened upon myself and my escort; down we went into the water at once. They asserted that the bullets passed through the branches of a shrub beside us. I am not sure. In any case, I did not like it, as one of my men whom I had been speaking to a little earlier in the day was caught by the same gun and received three bullet wounds, one in the shoulder and two in the arm. But he will come all right in the end, I think. There was a good deal of shooting at my working parties with machine guns, so I knocked up my gunners about midnight and threw our shrapnel on to the Germans, and then they saw that I meant to be "top dog," and went home to bed, I suppose. However, they stopped worrying me, which was all I really wanted. I am trying the preparation issued by the Government as an experiment to keep one's feet warm. As a matter of fact, it does not seem to do so at all; possibly that may be the fault of my floor—what remains of it, at least! The red tiles, though clean, are very cold. Well, this stuff looks like shaving soap, but there is another thing, "whale oil," which none of us have as yet tried. The latter was given out to us last night, and sounds promising, but nasty. All the Channel swimmers rub themselves over with it before attempting to swim across the Channel. Speaking about the tiled floors, I notice in many cases that little holes are cut in the sides of the houses, so that the tiles can be well washed with water, and then it drains outside without further trouble, but think how draughty it makes the place unless a plug is put to close this hole at night, and by day too in cold weather. I also notice that these French houses show signs of natty niceness which one would not see in an English farmhouse. For instance, in my sleeping-room, instead of nails being driven into the walls for hanging clothes on, there is a brass hook with a china knob like any Christian household. I am rather amused to see how indifferent our men have grown to fire. This morning between 5 and 6 o'clock I was speaking to the sentry when a bullet came, hit the house, and gave a great streak of light, as it does when it strikes a hard substance. A large piece of the building fell down behind him, but he never changed his voice or paid the slightest attention. I have had a letter from your aunt at Rostrevor about Sydney, to whom she seems very devoted....

In Trenches.
January 24th, 1915.

I believe that to-day is Sunday, judging from the sound of church bells in the direction of the second town, which lies four miles behind us. They were ringing "to church" while we were standing "to arms" in the dark with a good deal of rifle fire, though not much from the guns. A new lot of Germans, we think, have come opposite to us, and they are very hard shooters, always firing either machine guns or rifles. We are too busy working at our parapets now to go for them, but when they are finished I propose to wake them up well. I got in rather early last night about midnight. You know war has comic incidents as well as pathetic ones. I was finishing my way round the trenches in the dark, when Mr. Gartland, R.I.R., a very nice boy, attached himself to me, and said he had orders to go to a certain place and did not know the road, and might he come with me. Of course I said "Yes," and we progressed till we came to a bridge, just a plank really over a wide stream. I crossed it quietly after whispering to him to be careful. Next moment I heard a frantic struggle and fall, and discovered him clutching on for dear life to the plank, having slipped on it. We managed to rescue him from a watery grave. I must tell you that all of this was out in the open within 200 yards of the German trenches, as we were crossing from company to company. My escort also fell at this bridge, but I caught him by the scruff of the neck, thereby preventing him getting into the water. I suppose Oakfield, my old home in Nova Scotia, taught me a bit about roughing it, so, elderly man that I am, I can keep fairly steady on my feet over this tricky ground. Well, having safely delivered Mr. G. at his place, I moved on, when we heard another fearful splash and then more floundering, and found that a corporal of my stretcher-bearers had fallen into a very deep drain full of water. Again my escort and myself started off to earn the Royal Humane Society's medal. However, he managed to scramble out, wet through. As I say, the comic side alternates with the pathetic, for just then we had a poor boy shot through the head. In the dark we made out that it was his eye, but on getting him to hospital, where we could strike a light to work with, we saw that the bullet had gone through the nose, down the side of the face, and out through his neck. He is alive this morning, so it may be that he will turn the corner all right yet. I received your letter of January 20th last night, which is good. You ask me about block houses. They are only useful when screened from artillery fire. If we had one here, and the Germans could place it with glasses or with aeroplanes, they would blow it up at once. They were used largely in the South African War, because we had taken all the enemy's guns from him. Sorry to hear of your cold. Hope the Kaiser has a very bad one with a sore throat!!...

In Trenches.
January 25th, 1915.

I was sorry to see by your note in pencil yesterday that you were in bed with "Flu." I hope you will not have it very badly, and that you are up again and all right by this time. There has been a good deal of trouble lately with German machine guns playing on our working parties at night. So yesterday afternoon I crept off unobserved, and had a conclave with my gunners.

Then when they started with their guns I had all the adversary's trenches mapped out, and dropped four shells on them. About an hour later they began again, but we squelched them in the same way; finally they stopped firing their horrid machines and remained quiet; not for long, however, for they next turned their heavy guns on us in the dark with the high explosive shell. The first burst about 100 yds. away, and the second nearer, whilst the third burst alongside the house. I wailed, expecting one in the ruins, but they fired no more, thank heavens! The last scattered everything all over the house, bricks, tiles, etc. I was curled up in a blanket at that hour ready to go over the whole of the trenches, having arranged to start between three and four o'clock this morning. I got round all right with, if anything, fewer bullets than usual flying about. A message has just been sent to us that an attack is expected on our right, so we are now waiting to see whether this comes to anything or not. The day is particularly dark, though so far no rain or snow. It is quite black enough for the latter, but not, perhaps, sufficiently cold. I am rather sleepy at present, and I hate getting up early. To-night we go into support, which means that some of our companies, now 600 yds. from the enemy, will be in a position farther back, but this threatened attack may make a difference. Another regiment, the Royal Berkshires, are alongside of us, and we always go into the trenches and come out together. The Colonel is senior to me, and is commanding the Brigade in the General's absence, so the next senior takes his regiment. The latter was knocked over by a shot two days ago. He only broke his hip, and it is expected to come right in due course. Do you remember Miss Arundel's nephew, Capt. Wickham, of the 7th Fusiliers, who went out with me to India, half-brother to Sir Henry Tichborne, I believe? I saw three days ago that he had died of wounds; so they must have brought him home from India. I am sorry; he and I had many pleasant chats together on board ship. Would you look in the upper left-hand drawer in my dressing-room. You will find some stand-up single collars there with five buttonholes in them. Please roll one up flat, and send it across in a letter or with soap parcel. They go in collar of uniform jacket, and as this sort of collar has gone out, I am wearing mine and throwing them away when done.

In Billets.
January 26th, 1915.

I am very sorry that you have been obliged to send for the doctor. "Flu" makes one feel a worm, so take care of yourself. I do not fancy you need fear the air raids; keep to the country, it is safer than town. They have not enough explosives on their cars to do all the damage they would like in London, let alone the remainder of England. The trip to Norfolk was only a trial one, I think. It has turned very cold here now, and we cannot get a fire in this place. You see, the inhabitants are coming back, and we do not like to steal their wood, for it would cause unpleasantness, whilst we have great difficulty in getting any coal, so we are between the devil and the deep sea! The Germans managed to kill one man yesterday with their shelling. I mean one civilian, of course; soldiers do not count. I suppose we are fair targets. I have been very lucky, though, with my Batt., on the whole, for I have only had a quarter of the casualties of my neighbour the two last times, or even less. Of course, it is just luck, but I take every precaution, as you know, and use my guns on their machine guns in, I hope, a judicious manner, giving the gunners little maps of where we have spotted them along all our long front; and so we crush the scamps. They are a venomous crew. They marked a bridge that we cross over a ditch, consisting of two planks and a hand-rail, and they turned their Maxims on to that. A couple of men were there, and they lay down on the bridge whilst the Maxim fired over their heads, cut the hand-rail clean away, and just missed them. We got off quite well from the trenches last night, as the enemy had had a great doing down with us that afternoon. The threatened attack on our right either never came off or was also beaten off; let us hope the latter. So dear old Admiral Dennistoun has gone. At 78 one must expect to go to Heaven shortly, but still one's friends will be sorry, no doubt, and Hal loses his godfather. I did not know him very well myself, but I am sorry because you were fond of him. I wonder if it is about to settle in for cold weather in these parts. If so, we shall have attacks across the frozen ground. Whilst it was wet the Germans could not very well get at us without giving plenty of notice, but now they will be able to work their way quietly across the hard earth. However, it cuts in another way, for they are not too well clothed and they will feel this severe weather terribly. It is horrible always to have to hope that many Germans will be killed. On the whole, it is more charitable to pray, I think, that the heart of the German nation may be turned to the right course. I fancy that the people are a sober, steady race, but they have been led astray by their warlike leaders. Again, who would imagine that the light French character (speaking generally as a nation) really covers a hard-working set of prosperous farmers like these people evidently are. Well, I hope you will be out of bed when this reaches you. I have not been able to write to the children lately, for there has been much to do and think about. Give them my love; thank your mother for the partridges so kindly sent, and can you let me have some more boxes of Bryant and May's matches? About 1,000; I fancy our men would be glad of them now. You will be able to find out through Bryant and May's how to get them across. The price is 21s., but I think they send them by the M.F.O., Southampton. Perhaps the best way would be to despatch the first half to me by post and the other lot by M.F.O., as the latter would arrive a month later when required again....

I have just received a telephone message that the Germans did attack, and were repulsed, losing heavily. They left 3 officers and 300 men dead on one road alone from our fire. Hope our losses are light.

In Billets.
January 27th, 1915.

Sorry to hear from your letter that you are still in bed. I do not see as much of my own bed as I would like to at present, but this thing has to be seen through. Being the Kaiser's birthday, we anticipated an attack, so to cheer our friends up and to show them what they might expect we opened on them at 5 o'clock this morning with our heavy guns. Such a row you never heard. The unbroken panes of glass in my room have long ago had all the putty shaken out and they rattle away to any extent when the guns are fired. It is very cold and chilly over here now, but not freezing, and we are rejoicing in the defeat of the Germans. They appear to be better at killing women and children with their men-of-war than fighting our ships when they meet them. I must say I have a poor opinion of them, not of their fighting qualities, but because they behave so badly. Curiously enough, the enemy never replied to our bombardment. It was directed on our right front, where poor Bannon, my servant, whom you will remember in Dover, was killed, and where we think these beauties gather in the mornings and stand to arms. It was a good bombardment. If some of them were about, there must be a lot killed. I did all I could to cheer everyone on. Well, I went for a ride yesterday after discussing your most excellent partridges at lunch, and saw my new draft. I am very strong, despite my losses, and I would like to show you my battalion when it first came out of the trenches and a month afterwards; you would see the difference! We are about twice as strong as the regiment was under Col. Napier at Dover. I heard from Admiral Gaunt yesterday. He has just been promoted, and is in charge of naval barracks. I must write him a note this morning. Wonderful people the French women! They are like cats the way they cling to their homes. The lady of this house has now returned, small baby and all, and has asked for two rooms. Having succeeded, she has got an old attempt at a carpenter in, and is boarding up the broken windows, etc. The bullet hole in the door will puzzle him unless he stops it up with a cork. Anyhow, they are making a most horrible din, banging away. I forgot to say that yesterday my Mother sent me from Oakfield two pairs of thick strong socks and some Canadian chocolate. Most useful, and very kind. I shall write soon to thank her.

In Billets.
January 28th, 1915.

This being our last rest day, I was out shortly after five o'clock with our acting General inspecting a new work. It is not healthy to do so much later in the day. We found two shell holes in it as it was, and the thing is only traced out, not made as yet. For Lady Bell's address [the Governor of Aden's wife] you will find a book giving it in my despatch case. Please send her my history as promised. I heard from Lady Macready yesterday, full of life as usual. She and I have been friends for a very long time, and we used to ride together in Egypt years ago. Sir Nevil has been motoring round the south of France inspecting Indian rest camps, and spent two days at Avignon on leave. I managed to obtain the Distinguished Conduct Medal for the bugler who always accompanies me everywhere on my peregrinations. He has been with me through some nasty times, though nothing to talk about very much, and I am glad to be able to reward him. Besides, it is good for the men to find that any work well done under my own eye may win them some recognition. I was out for a scamper yesterday afternoon inspecting my transport. This latter, by-the-by, has been very favourably reported on as the best looked after in the division (I am told). It is flattering, but one never knows! My Brigadier also complimented me on the smartness of my guards at Brigade Headquarters. If you saw the poor dears crawling out of the trenches, caked with mud and numbed with wet and cold, you could not understand how they could turn themselves out fairly decently twenty-four hours later, when they only have the one suit they are actually wearing all the time. I have not heard if the Saddler's Company proposes to send me any coffee, but I expect to hear in due course. As to the numb feeling in one's feet, one never has time to rub oneself over with Bengue's ointment. It will have to stand until the summer, I expect. The cake has duly arrived, and is tucked away until to-night, when we arrive in our trenches again, worse luck!...

In Trenches.
January 29th, 1915.

No letter from you last night; it must have missed the mail; but there were several others. One from the dentist; please put it in my drawer at home for reference. Another letter was from Mabel Stevens saying that Percy was home again with a bad leg; and yet a third was from the remount officer who bought my horse for the Government, telling me that he is afraid the chestnut "Goldfinch" has been mixed up with some horses at Southampton and given out to other people. So ends poor "Goldfinch's" career as far as I am concerned. We hear some amusing reports from the prisoners on our right. They say we took 2 officers and 80 men, besides killing a large number of the 7,000 who attacked our particular trench; also that the Germans expect to beat the Russian Army in May, and that we have 150,000 Japanese soldiers holding India for us! I never heard this before, nor anyone else either! I fancy they were freely plied with ration rum, no doubt someone else going short, and thus their original opinions were found out. Last night was beautifully clear, with a moon. About 2 a.m. we became aware that a party of the enemy were out in front of us only 50 yds. away, so we stealthily gathered our men up and opened a rapid fire on them. They fled to their trenches for dear life, and have been very vicious ever since. One of my men was shot internally just now. I have got him away in a motor ambulance in the hopes that an operation may save his life. I was told yesterday that Gen. Joffre said the war would be over in March, he thought, from financial reasons. (I wonder?) The other story I heard last night in the trenches was that Rothschild met Kitchener and asked him when his army was going across. K. replied: "250,000 in February, and 250,000 in March." R. replied: "The 250,000 in February will go, but there will be no reason for sending the 250,000 in March." Of course, this is quite an improbable story, and K. would never really tell R. anything, and R. would never repeat it. Anyhow, my line is fairly strong, so that if it is not over they will not break through *here*. I am sitting facing a window with a bright sun shining; two of the enemy shells have just come over and burst. They each threw a shadow as they passed. I have never seen that before. They fired a lot at us yesterday. One six-inch howitzer sent a shell 50 yds. from us. We of course seized the pieces as new playthings, and found first a horrible odour arising from some acid in their high explosive, and then that the shell appeared to be cast only of iron, and not steel. The piece I have in front of me weighs about a pound, with dreadful jagged edges. So soon as this shelling stops I must sneak off to try and put our cemeteries straight. I am having some very nice wooden crosses made for my poor men. Do tell me how Mr. Denison is? He might be interested in some of this news, as he was a gunner, and it is all about shells, if ever I get home to tell him! In the middle of this shelling both sides firing hard at each other, one of my buglers has arrived with a carrier pigeon which was knocked down by a stone. The French officer attached to our division told me that the Germans had spent large sums of money and established many spies as farmers here. They intended coming in this way to France, you see. Then they had telephone wires laid down towards Germany from various places, and I am inclined to think some have been found. Now our numerous trenches having cut these wires, they have to depend on something else, and I believe that something to be carrier pigeons. The way they shell the ground we occupy makes me think they really know where we are, and our own military authorities do not like to take drastic action against a person who poses as a French farmer or his wife looking for their lost property, when of course all the time they are possibly farmers who have been in German pay, and are probably sending information across by carrier pigeon daily. I hope that Wilkinson in Newark is making a good thing of the steel armour. It is rather a fine trophy to have, I think....

P.S.—I discovered our gunners shelling a beautiful French cemetery the other day, because the Germans had found that we respected churches, etc., and they therefore opened the vaults and lived in them in the cemetery!

In Trenches.
January 30th, 1915.

Two letters from you last night, taking me up to January 27th. So glad to hear that you are really better. I do not know what would happen to us if we got "Flu." I suppose we should go on exactly the same. One of the enemy's six-inch shells has just burst beside us, so I must keep my eyes open! I started work soon after five o'clock this morning getting road dykes cleared, as by this means I think I can drain my own trenches better. The water has been running away merrily ever since. Major B———, who came back about one o'clock this morning, was helping me. I had just turned in, but my feet got so cold. I can never sleep straight on end for four hours in my room. The Germans again attacked on our right twice yesterday afternoon. The two attacks were beaten off with heavy loss to the enemy, I believe. I was out with one of my staff inspecting some works, and met the Colonel of the Lincolns with his staff. I asked him to tea, and he refused on the ground that "shelling time" had arrived, and he did not wish to go near our Headquarters. Whilst he trotted off to inspect one work, I went to another, and sure enough he was quite right. "Shelling time" had arrived; for, instead of going for my Headquarters as usual, they proceeded to shower shrapnel on the work he had just got into, fortunately, without killing or hurting any of his party. Our guns are now replying, and bits of our ruin are falling down from the shock. Poor Gen. Baron von Ompteda! He was in the Prussian Army. It is sad that he is killed, since you knew his wife, poor thing! Naturally one prays for the heart of the German nation to be changed, but for me, pending that change, I am doing my business methodically. I have just been pointing out to the Siege Battery people where their shells will have the best effect on the enemy. I forgot, I think, to tell you that we obtained information from some of our prisoners of the last three days that they found our rifle fire very deadly. Well, one of the regiments that attacked us had already lost from our fire 320 men since January 20th only until the 27th inst.... Not bad, and quite true, I believe; and this going on all along the line. There was bright moonlight last night with snow, and I may tell you that I walked warily! I had one man killed and another wounded by the same bullet yesterday....

In Trenches.
January 31st, 1915.

 I am now waiting for your letter to-night. I cut from *The Times* of January 29th "Soldiers' Morals" and Lady McClintock's views. Major Baker brought this paper across with him when he returned. Well, it is trying to snow now, and rather cold. Yesterday I came under the fire of a machine gun in the course of my afternoon rounds. I had gone to see some works that the Artillery were building and which I had to supervise. Hearing a fight break out on our right, I called to the Engineers who were working on the parapets to jump down, as the machine gun which was near us might be turned on them. They had barely done so, and I had hardly gone forward with an officer to get some other men under cover, when the next moment the bullets were whistling all over me. I soon flew from that spot at the first crash, and got under cover myself; a quick decision does help one at times! After being pinned there for ten minutes or so, I managed to creep away and get on with my rounds. There has been a cannonade on my right all morning of the heaviest Gunner shells, I think, but we luckily go into reserve this evening, and, failing any great alarms, are allowed to have our boots off, and do not get up at 5 a.m. as usual. Another curious incident occurred. Suddenly we heard the most appalling noise, and the shell of one of our own heavy guns was seen turning head over heels and falling solemnly within 50 yds. of a ruin where some 100 soldiers were quartered. It burst and sent any amount of rubbish over the house. What happened was that part of the shell was defective. It really was the driving band, which is a ring made out of copper and riveted on. When the shell is fired, the soft copper ring slides into the steel rifling of the gun, and thus the shell goes straight with a spinning motion. The ring having become unriveted, the shell did not spin, and simply turned head over heels. Was it not fortunate that it missed the house? It is because they have no copper for these rings that the Germans are making such strenuous efforts to find some. Nothing else except silver or gold would be tough enough as well as pliable enough for the purpose. They can make their fuses of aluminium as we do, but copper for cartridge cases and driving bands they must have, and they cannot get it....

LETTERS OF FEBRUARY, 1915.

In Billets.
February 1st, 1915.

My dearest F——

Here we are in our reserve billets, and not sorry either. The enemy threw a shell in beside us this morning as I was getting up, to show that he had not forgotten us! It must have come 5 miles at least. He is a humorist, too, of a grim sort, for 3 days ago he bombarded the little town (French) of Estaires with French shells. I suppose some gun he had captured from them. Anyhow, his ammunition is certainly, as a rule, not as good as the stuff he was using. Have a headache this morning. I often get one after 3 days in trenches. There was a great hue and cry after a German spy yesterday. Telephones going all over the place. I was wickedly sceptical about him from the first, and ultimately triumphantly proved him to be an officer of the —— Regiment who had been detached on some duty. The unfortunate gentleman had an impediment in his speech, and this was noted down as proving him to be a German, of course! Six divisions of K.'s new army are expected to cross over to France this month. I hear that the Canadians have also arrived, and that they are full of dash. Thanks for collars, duly received. They will last me a long time. Major Baker brought some mincepies back with him. Mr. Argles wonders if I have time to see any of the sports out here! No one has the least idea of how busy one is out of the trenches getting rifles right and men cleaned to keep them from dirt whilst in the trenches, when it is impossible to do anything, for you cannot lift your head there for fear of having it punctured before you pull it down again.... You ask if I have seen any of my relatives who are at the front. No. I think they are all farther back, and if they should come up where I am they would have an awful time of it.... I hear the whirr of an aeroplane. I wonder if it is ours or a German bomb dropper; you never know which it may be! So glad to hear you are feeling better.

Yours....
G——

February 2nd, 1915.

I must say that I think quite the worst news we have received so far in this war is the sinking of those three ships in the Irish Sea by the German submarines. The British Navy must just get to work and build a submarine destroyer which will catch and destroy these nuisances. As a matter of fact, I believe a great many more German submarines have been sunk than the British public know of, because it is not announced unless the Admiralty is absolutely certain. For instance, the other day an old naval carpenter who works on the Bayfordbury Estate in Hertfordshire, and who returned to his naval duties when the war broke out, told Major Baker that whilst dragging for mines in the German Ocean they had come against two submarines lying on the bottom of the sea, and, having nothing else to do, they dropped a charge on them and blew them up. That may be correct or not. I have certainly heard that this happened in one case, officially. A long letter from my sister Meta arrived by the last post yesterday; still moving into Oakfield after building up the old house again since the fire. I went for a ride yesterday with Major B., looking up some roads in case of a move. The Germans tried to pour shrapnel on the road on the way back, but fortunately missed us by going short. There was a large party of another division on it, and I suppose they had got wind of this. A curious thing to notice is as follows: When a shell starts out on its journey it travels more quickly than the sound. Sound moves at the rate of about a mile in 5 seconds. After a little while the shell begins to go more slowly, and then the sound overtakes it and travels ahead. We were just where we could see the shell burst with a flash and a white puff of smoke, and could still hear the whirr of the shell rushing towards us until it ended with a loud bang, though we had in reality seen it burst a second or so before. We went to a rather fine church destroyed by fire. I asked what had happened, and was told that the Germans had been there, and when they were forced to retreat they put a certain number of their dead inside the church with a lot of straw, then some of the villagers, and finally made one of the women set fire to the straw by holding a revolver to her head and threatening to shoot her. The man said that the village priest had told him this shocking story. I asked how the Germans had behaved otherwise, and he said, "Very well in one sense." They had been billeted on the people, who were obliged to feed them; but, of course, it is war. When, however, they had to retire, they refused to pay for anything, and tried, as the inhabitants explained, to incite them with a view of getting an excuse to burn their houses and then shoot them. As the village people kept their heads, they threw down half a mark and left. I thought, on the whole, they were well rid of their visitors! You asked if I required any more soap or paper. At present, nothing, thanks; Major B—— has just given me a new writing block. A cake and mincepies are, however, always most welcome. How greedy one does become after a time! Such a horrid blustery day, and heavy rain coming down this morning. We had Holy Communion at 8 a.m. in a ruined nunnery with our Cowley Father officiating. Only 3 turned up from the whole Battalion. Our

General has had to go away this morning into hospital with fever. Mr. Laing, whom your cousin M—— D—— asked about, is now in bed with the same sort of complaint....

February 3rd, 1915.

We are off to the trenches this evening, worse luck! but we can't complain, for we have had a most comfortable 3 days considering everything; actually sleeping until 8 o'clock in the morning, washing ourselves and clothes, and generally doing ourselves well by buying eggs, butter, and wine of sorts. White wine appears to be the most plentiful in this locality—why, I cannot tell. It is a sort of Grave, and not at all bad as things go. Major B—— and I rode yesterday, despite the rain, and on the way we went to a place I have rigged up where my pioneer sergeant is making crosses for those who have been killed. Very nice wooden ones, which have little plates on them, also of wood, with name and so forth painted in black, standing about 2 ft. 6 in. high. The men admire them very much indeed, and I fancy that they like me to take an interest. It raises their self-respect. I found that, although some have already been put up, 16 crosses were standing there waiting for white and black paint, as we had run short of it, and these sort of things are difficult to get. The sugar I bought here for the men is 7d. a lb., and it is greatly appreciated by them. Of course, it is not allowed to be imported from England during the war, otherwise we might get it cheaper. I am glad you had a nice day for your first outing; as you say, "Flu" is very nasty. I wonder if I shall be able to run over again in March and see you. The Colonel of our gunners has just dashed in to ask me to luncheon before I go to the trenches. He says that he wants cheering up. I suppose he thinks me an optimist! What time would suit you best if I could get a week at the end of February or beginning of March? I know you said something about running across to Ireland again, and I do not wish to interfere with that. I do not know whether I shall be able to get it, but it is an idea. I see the Kaiser is in Berlin—the newspaper says "with his throat." I believe he is really there seeing if he can raise another loan, which will tax his ingenuity. He will announce in the papers that he has succeeded all right; but I think it will only be paid up in his own banknotes, which, of course, unless he has gold to redeem them, are worthless....

In Trenches.
February 4th, 1915.

We returned here last night. Before leaving the billets I was going round putting things right, when suddenly German shrapnel began bursting over my head. I hustled my men under cover, and no one was hurt, though a shrapnel broke the window in the house where we were and came through it. We started off cheerfully enough, and arrived at our trenches safely by 7 p.m. There was heavy firing on our right, and at about 9 o'clock the German guns opened, putting shell all round us, including one in the house next to us about 20 yds. away. Of course it is only ruined walls, but it made a tremendous crack. The house is rather a nice one of fresh red brick with bright red tiles on the roof, and it also has blue and white glazed tiles over the doors and windows. We then made ourselves horribly obnoxious with our machine guns, and opened by arrangement. You never heard such a noise. As a matter of fact, we knew that they were changing regiments at that hour, and we tried to catch them with our artillery. Whether we succeeded I cannot tell. I have been up and about since between 2 and 3 a.m., so one earns one's bread out here! The machine guns were particularly busy, but there was hardly a shot fired at me in all my rounds! This morning two German aeroplanes arrived. One of ours had been playing about, but it fled when the enemy appeared. We fired on them immediately, and they went off. Then ours came round again, and the Germans reappeared, but it did not run away so fast, and we again helped it. Now two of ours are sailing up and down, shot at by German infantry, their own aeroplanes having vanished. From two different German sources we learn that they expect the war to be over in April, as they have told the troops that Russia is beaten. Some have admitted that they hardly expect their troops will fight after April; but from my knowledge of Germans I do not think they will be given the option; they will be shot by the authorities if they do not fight. We have also had the cheerful news that, regiment for regiment, their casualties are about four times our number. This I believe to be correct. I had a pleasant little lunch with the Colonel of the Gunners, and a whisky and soda, which I have not tasted before in France so far....

In Trenches.
February 5th, 1915.

Not up quite so early this morning, as my acting General said he was coming round, and I had to meet him at a certain point, so I did not rise much before four a.m. We went about until 7 o'clock, doing various things, fortunately with very little shooting. There was a heavy bombardment last night from our guns at 10 o'clock, but I do not think it did the enemy a great deal of harm, and we fired at him again with big guns in the morning. He is trying to approach us by a sap, and we are trying to blow him out of it. Not that we object to his coming close, but because he wants to enter that particular place; so it is right that he should at once be sternly checked. I received two of your letters last night, dated the 1st and the 2nd. I am sorry about the death of your cousin, Mrs. Hilton; but her heart had undoubtedly been weak for sometime. C—— S—— must have been grieved that he did not arrive in time to see her again. Tell him I am in sympathy with him over his loss. Thanks for sending me a cake. The eggs do not really do us much good now, as we have found out a way of getting them. I had a kind letter from my Mother last night promising me two more pairs of socks and some more chocolate. I wish I could put on three pairs of socks here, as my feet are always cold. The ruins of the French houses have their floors covered with tiles, as I think I told you before, and they are cold to the feet. Unfortunately feet swell, and boots even two sizes too large appear to shrink, so finally one thick pair of socks is possible only. I heard from the Saddlers' Coy. yesterday that they propose to send me the coffee and milk, and that my letter had been read to the full Court and had been found very interesting. I heard also from General Inglefield; he says that he would like me to have a Brigade before long.

In Trenches.
February 6th, 1915.

The Generals gave out yesterday that we were to be attacked last night, the reason being that the Germans were seen to be clearing the wire away from their trenches, presumably with this plan in view. We decided to discourage any such attempts by opening the affair ourselves. We therefore fired on them with all sorts of things, including an iron drain pipe which throws a ring of gun cotton. This is simply made out of an old jam tin, whilst the fuse is lit before firing the charge in the drain-pipe. The latter charge of powder is then driven out of the jam tin. If correctly judged, it hurtles through the air and falls into the German trenches, and blows people there to pieces. How close the fire is here is shown by one of my companies having had two periscopes hit. Periscopes are four inches wide or less, and probably only 5 inches shows above the parapet, so you can see the German marksman at 100 yds. anyhow is not to be despised. This morning I was up before four o'clock, and round my men. On my way back a German put a bullet between the Corporal and myself. Of course lots of others were flying about, but this was the nearest. We go into support to-night; and the house we are going to occupy had a shell through the front door two days ago. It was fired at from the side at some great distance, came through the door, and fell on its back without exploding just short of a cupboard. This must have come from a strange battery, as the ordinary shells go round it all and every day, bursting galore, so I suppose this was one up the line fired at a sharp angle to try and take us in flank, as it were. I am rather sleepy, as there was a fire fight at 12 p.m. last night, for which I was awake. I received a letter from Miss Ruby McCann of Belfast yesterday, sending tobacco and her love to the men. The latter, she stated, was only to the "good-looking ones." I also had a letter from your Mother. She told me that you had not gone to the concert owing to A—— H——'s death that very day. Still, of course, you took tickets for it. I also received a note from the Saddlers' Co. saying that they were sending four cans of milk and coffee to me to start with, and more would follow when they heard how the men liked it. The cans have four dozen tins in each. Very kind indeed of them. Well, I think that is all my news, excepting that I have got a headache, and have had one for the last two days, which is not surprising, since I have been up and about at such unearthly hours, and have not had any chance of sleeping properly in between whiles. I am always on the telephone to one person or the other....

In Billets.
February 7th, 1915.

I hear that Col. Napier has got a Brigade, and I must write to congratulate him. You are kind in offering to send us more cakes and mincepies. What we really miss according to our usual mode of life is the absence of the "sweet" course at luncheon or dinner. Perfectly ridiculous! Just the same as washing, but one misses it somehow, that is all, even when one is eating covered with mud. I received your letter of February 3rd last night; usually these letters only take 2 days to come. Thanks for sending Bryant and May's matches. I hope they will arrive shortly via Southampton. Tell Blanche I am sorry for her troubles with her teeth: I am trying to see a dentist myself. I hear there is one at a little distance away, and I propose to ride over to see him to-morrow, if possible. We go across to a canal, and follow that for 8 miles, and then he, the dentist, is to be found somewhere in an ambulance. A very good thing to be able to get away from under shell fire even for a short time. We had rather a doing yesterday, for the Germans shelled us heavily, and finally concentrated on two houses. Curiously enough, I had pointed out to the authorities how very visible some works the Engineers had constructed were to the enemy from their aircraft, and I stated that the woodwork ought to be painted earth colour, and sent out a party of men in the meantime to cover the wood with mud. Unfortunately, however, the mud dried, leaving the wood still rather light, and the aircraft came along all right, as I suspected, saw it, and signalled to their gunners where to fire. By some good luck, the 2 houses alongside, though they were full of my men, had also shelters erected to protect them from shell fire. These they ran into, and so escaped; only Major W—— was hit on the head by a splinter, which did not hurt him, as his skull is fairly resisting! The few remaining rafters were blown off the houses and the walls fell down. It was most unpleasant to stand by helplessly and watch it; I could not turn on our gunners, for a very heavy bombardment was going on to our right at the usual place which I have mentioned to you before. The shells we captured were French, and exploded well. Coming out of the trenches, the company that came my way had one corporal killed and one wounded. The poor man was shot dead just before leaving the trenches. I quickened our pace up, I can tell you, when we suddenly found ourselves walking along in the line of a hot fire fight in front of us; though it was a mile and a half away in the darkness, one bullet struck beside me, and another went over my head. The shell which struck this house was evidently nearly spent, and the broken door is just like the back entrance of your aunt's house opposite Carlton church. It went clean through this; then turned to the right through a thick wall and landed in a cupboard on a shelf, smashing the doors, but not exploding....

In Billets.
February 8th, 1915.

Very heavy rain last night, and plenty of mud this morning after five o'clock, when we stood to arms. I am going to Merville, as I said, this afternoon to get my teeth looked to. I took Major B. for a longish walk yesterday. He hates walking, but brightened up considerably as we went along, and we talked of our various troubles. We have certain worries with some of our men who have not been brought up in the strict discipline really required for a continental war. Cheering news has come to us from Russia. A General was sent by the Czar to decorate Sir John French and the Colonel of the Scots Greys, of which the Czar is Col. in chief. He is reported to have said: "Do not worry; we have not yet mobilized in Russia, but we shall do so in the beginning of April, and we do not ask you to do more than wait here holding the enemy; then we propose simply to march on Berlin with overwhelming numbers." So be it, as long as we get these thieves settled soon. That heavy fighting I told you about La Bassée way, going on two days ago, was our storming a German trench; I hear that we killed a lot of Germans and captured 30. Of course we must have lost heavily ourselves too. Would you send a copy of my History, of which you have already sent two away, to Col. Anderson, Headquarters, VIII Division, B.E.F. His father was in the regiment, and he is interested in it. Also to my Mother please send a copy with my love. By the way, all parcels to France are expensive, but if the postage by chance is not fully paid it does not matter, as no extra charge is made at this end. Now I must stop, as I am as busy as possible to-day trying to get things done, and everyone wants to see me at once. Such a lovely sun!...

In Billets.
February 9th, 1915.

Well, I went yesterday afternoon and had two teeth filled, one under the gum, which is still rather painful; but the amusing point is that on my way there at some cross roads I was held up for a quarter of an hour by the Germans shelling the place. I hid in a building, and when they got off the line of the road I resumed my ride on to my dentist. Just at this moment they are shelling our usual front line billets vigorously. I mean the ruined houses which we hide behind. Clearly they must have got more ammunition. Many thanks for cake, chocolate, tins of coffee and cocoa, and boiled eggs, which all arrived safely. As a matter of fact, the cake is most useful, whilst we still have a fair amount of chocolate, and the eggs please do not send again, for we have now a regular system of supplying eggs to ourselves at 3-½ francs a dozen, which keeps us going. I am glad the children like reading and receiving my letters. Sometimes I am rather hustled for time, as I have often a great deal to do, and many of my officers have not been on active service before. First, you have to think out the orders, and then issue them in writing, and then, still more important, see that they are carried out. Sorry to hear of Miss Dunlop's death; she has gone to a better world, anyhow. The one she has left is in a troublous condition. Please God, it soon rights itself! No soup squares required, please. I fancy that if I get my leave at all it will be before April, but of course I cannot choose the time or anything like that. In fact, they may refuse to allow me to have a second leave. Had a letter from Bertha Farmar; she is full of news, and seems very happy. I do not know anything about Colonels only going into the trenches at night. I have been in during the day often; but in the trenches that we now occupy it is carrying your life in your hand to do so—that is, for a tall man; once in, it is just a question of bending down. It is strange to hear of people playing football out here—we ourselves are under fire every minute. One of our men was hit yesterday on the head by a German bullet four hundred yards farther down the street from where I live, whilst he was having his hair cut by the company barber. We had fondly imagined that we were out of the way of bullets!

Yours....

We go into our trenches again to-night, worse luck!

In Trenches.
February 10th, 1915.

Here we are back in the trenches, and a shell has just burst quite close to us. A Yeomanry major has been lunching with me. I put him up in the "Residency" at Aden on his way home, and he asked to come down into our trenches, though he belongs to another division, as he wanted the experience. His name is Backhouse, and his brother was Flag Lieutenant to Admiral Jellicoe at the beginning of the war. We arrived here very peacefully last night, cheered by news of the Russian successes, and then I went my rounds from 3 o'clock till 7.30 in the morning. I pointed out to some of my men that they were standing in a dangerous place, but they said it was all right, and I heard an hour after that three of them had been struck by one bullet. Later the General came along to see about things, and I had to go round with him. A shrapnel from our guns burst short and just missed a man I was speaking to.... However, thank Heaven! we did not have any fired at us. A curious thing happened the night before last. One of the British patrols in my line saw a German at the wire entanglements in the darkness, and fired. The German fell, calling out: "Don't shoot, soldier." When they were able to get up to him they found that he had laid his rifle and equipment down before he was seen, and either wanted to surrender or, as he had some wire cutters with him, was trying to cut the entanglement. Anyhow, poor fellow! he had had the large artery of his leg cut, and was just at the point of death. We buried him at the back of the ruin. Did you ever think how between the devil and the deep sea the German soldier is? If he runs away, he is shot; if he advances, he is generally shot; and if he tries to desert, as in this case, he is shot too. A hard fate....

In Trenches.
February 11th, 1915.

Getting up at 3 a.m. is very trying, as it makes the day so long. I curl up in my blankets at 9 p.m., and hope for the best, but very often I am pulled out again. Last night, for instance, we had various parties down here working during the night. About 8 o'clock I went to look at the poor German's grave, and, coming away from it, I was nearly hit by a bullet from some sniper who was evidently watching me. I am just waiting to go to one of our own men's funeral. He was shot yesterday, poor boy! and I was able to get his body out, so I am trying to give all such, decent burial with a clergyman some distance back from the trenches. I forgot to tell you when mentioning that shrapnel shell yesterday that the man I was talking to was Sergeant Driscoll, whom you will remember in the regiment; and that a sergeant of the Lincolns was killed in my lines exactly the same way the day before. I enclose Mr. Aitchison's letter. I did not realize that it was his only son. I heard from Mrs. Baker yesterday in reply to a letter of mine. She compliments you on your letters, saying you are quite a soldier's wife.... I calculate that I might, but only might, get away about February 28th for a week if nothing turns up in the interval; but, again, I was told that all leave was stopped in the 7th Division, so I am doubtful what will happen. Perhaps the war will end soon. Who knows?...

In Trenches.
February 12th, 1915.

Your letter not come yet, but posts do not always fit. We had a couple of amusements yesterday. One was the opening of fire from quite a new direction by the Germans. Fortunately, not very heavy, though. The other thing was that our house caught fire last night about 5.30. Major B. and the sergeant-major made the discovery. It originated with the guard, who, of course, were the last to find it out! Major B. and the Sgt. Major were both invaluable, but my first business was to see that the sentry was alert, so that we could carry on our operations without being surprised by our opponents. Next I got a ladder from a ruin, put a man up it with a hose, and said: "There are great gaping holes in the tiles everywhere; pull off the remaining ones, and then we can pour water all over the fire." There were very few, however, left to pull off, so the work was done and the fire put out in a few minutes. Lucky for us it was just before dark and the light just right, otherwise we should have been shelled to pieces. We buried that poor fellow I spoke about yesterday afternoon with a parson, keeping my eyes lifted for rifle bullets all the while. I forgot to tell you I stopped an N.C.O. as I was coming down to the trenches 3 nights ago to speak to one of our men; immediately afterwards he was hit in the leg by a bullet. As it was long range, the bullet remained in his calf, and he went off in an ambulance to have it dug out. One of my poor men died also this morning; it was astonishing that he was alive at all, for yesterday a bullet hit him in the head and blew the back of his head off, and yet he remained alive and quite conscious without pain till 2 a.m. I have just had a visit from an artillery officer; he and I have concerted a plan of operations together. As his shells are very heavy, things ought to be bad for the Germans. How I hate this business of killing people who never wanted the war, and would go home if it were possible! Now, if I could have an innings at those who actually made the war and murdered the women and children, I would have quite a different tale to tell, but these poor creatures are set in a groove and are helpless to escape out of it.

In Billets.
February 13th, 1915.

We got away quietly from our trenches on the night of the 12th, I am thankful to say. It was so dark that I could not see the man in front of me, though I could touch him with my hand. I "came," as the Irish say, a great sprawl over a bridge across a ditch, the chief difficulty being to find my uniform cap in the darkness and mud, as, of course, one did not wish to give away where we were by even a flash from one's electric torch. However, here we are in billets once again, with the rain pouring down and guns roaring now all round us. I cannot quite make out whether any shells from the enemy are falling or not. Since we came they have blown down a small building on the other side of the road from where I am sitting, and sent a shell into the medical inspection room. This gives some idea of how powerful even one of their medium-sized shells is, for it went through five thick brick walls before it exploded. I hope I may get leave again presently, but there appears to be some trouble about a second lot. I shall, however, put a brave face on and demand it in the ordinary course, and see what I can do. I am told that Colonels who have finished their command are kept on commanding their regiments out here during the war, as they are badly needed just at present, so I do not know that I shall get a Brigade when my time is up, as it will be ere long. Of course, everything is at sixes and sevens. I hope you have already sent Col. Anderson the copy of my History which he asked for. I am glad that Colonel Farmar has done so well with Sir Horace Smith-Dorrien, as he is such a good fellow, and in all probability he will have a good career before him. I must be off.

In Billets.
February 14th, 1915.

A wet day yesterday, and a wild night; rain stopped now, and turning very cold. Pleasant for the trenches, but I anticipate cold weather up to the middle of April at least, and very bitter weather in March. The Germans seized the opportunity to shell us and knock down the house next to mine, laying out two of my men and a sergeant of the Berkshires. Fortunately none of them were killed. They smashed the roof up, so we went round to get safer billets for the men. The house we took was inhabited by a very rich old man, who said he kept a house to live in and a shop to work in, not to put soldiers in! Pleasant loyal fellow! We simply said that he would have 125 soldiers there within half an hour. However, we asked the men, and they said they preferred to stay where they were. I expect, as much as anything, they were too tired to move. Well, I rode out with Major Baker to the Northamptonshire Yeomanry. They were commanded by a Col. Wickham, of the Scots Guards, an old gentleman who joined the Guards in 1874. They told me the sad news that when they applied for their second leave, they were refused, so I am afraid it looks as if none of us will get it, which is more than a nuisance. I enclose a letter from Athelstan Riley; it will interest you. Major B. has been decidedly ill several times on this campaign, and I have literally ordered him to stay in bed to get better, as he would not do so otherwise. I should like, if it comes my way, to bring out a Brigade; I am all for it! Percy's regiment, the Scots Greys, are in the trenches at present having a hard time. Many thanks for the prospect of another plum pudding; and jam tartlets of some sort, not made with plums, might be very good. Apple tartlets, very sweet, well covered in at the top, would be perfectly splendid. I do not think we require many things now. A lot of cigarettes and tobacco have been sent to us lately....

In Billets.
February 15th, 1915.

Such a wet day yesterday. We had service about 11 a.m. in the conservatory of a convent which in some curious way has escaped being destroyed. The enemy were shelling the town, so I put a corporal on the watch to give notice as the shells drew nearer. However, after coming fairly close they stopped firing. In the afternoon I went to see about my crosses for graves. I get a certain number sent down most nights whilst we are in the trenches. We have now the sum total of our children's ages [about 20] coming to us to-morrow night, so we shall have something to do to put them all up. Of course, these are for my own men only. In our diggings we are constantly turning up the bodies of Indians or Frenchmen, or of a few Englishmen who have held our trenches before us, and have been buried at the back during the night. Very awful, but so is all war. We go in to-night again to our most objectionable duty. I had a letter from Bertha. Col. Farmar is now well established on the staff with Gen. Smith-Dorrien. S.D. is far and away one of the most capable of our Generals, I am told. I am so sorry to hear of Miss Webb's [of Newstead Abbey] sudden death from heart, just like her sister, Lady Chermside. Well, that is about all my news. I am off this morning to inspect our bomb-throwers. No doubt these nasty weapons are useful on occasions, but they are most dangerous to those who handle them. So, too, with us—that is, in our Brigade—they have only blown up four of themselves. None of my men have done so as yet, I am thankful to say....

In Trenches.
February 16th, 1915.

Here we arrived peacefully last night; I went through the whole of my lines in places up to my knees in mud, as usual! There is practically no news to give you, excepting that to-day the country looks very nice with a bright sun shining. We have heard heavy firing at Ypres, and do not know what it all means, but I am fairly ready for them, anyhow, if they wish to come. I also learnt that the Germans drove the Russians out of East Prussia, because the latter were short of ammunition, but that the Russians killed and wounded 100,000 Germans before they went. A few more such German "victories" ought to about finish these knaves! How I wish I was back in England and at home!...

February 17th, 1915.

Am really in full blast now. On Saturday I was summoned to ride 5 miles to a conference. The first person I saw there was Col. Farmar, who had just returned from a flying visit to England. It was pleasant meeting him again, though we had not much time for a private talk. The conference being over, I was whisked off in a motor with a General. We were driven by a French soldier who had been two years in London and 7 years in America. After lunch at his billet I was told to reconnoitre the trenches we were to occupy that evening; we came upon a French woman of the rich farmer class who had just had her servant killed, and herself and baby wounded by a German shell. Then we went on to the trenches, leaving the General behind, and taking a staff officer instead. I found that my Brigadier had arranged that I was to take over the front of something over two regiments. There were plenty of shells bursting around me, including five in the next house and lots of rifle fire. Well, by the evening I had gathered all the information I wanted to know, so went back in my motor. Meanwhile the Brigadier sent word that we were to go to the town of———. It was perfectly dark there on our arrival, and after proceeding with great care on account of the shell-holes in the streets I came to the only lighted place there was, which turned out to be a General's headquarters. Here I was allowed to sit by the fire for a few minutes to dry myself, after which I went off in the dark and rain to arrange billets for the Bn. Of course this is not really my business, but everything was so huggermugger that I thought I should get matters along that way. Arriving at 1 a.m., I put the men into deserted French houses. The inhabitants had fled, so I was informed by a French officer at the General's Headquarters, because the Germans had asked for 50,000 francs for an indemnity, and it was not paid in the given time. They, so he said, shot the mayor and an old man of 80 years and another; so if that is true the people just panicked! We were very comfortable barring sleeping on the floor and having to get up at 5 a.m. on a Sunday, and in snowy weather too! Well, that day I received the order to move, and finally got into our trenches at four-thirty last night in downpours of rain. As we approached these, a heavy fight was in progress, and we came under fire of the spent bullets. One of my very good boxers, poor chap! was hit in the jaw and died at once. I suppose it dislocated the spine. Then the Germans threw star shell on us, and turned a searchlight upon us as well, so altogether made themselves very unpleasant, whilst our own shells burst short just above our heads as we stood on the road. In the dark I sorted everyone out, had a confab. with the two C.Os., and then sent my troops off under officers as guides to their trenches. I need hardly tell you that I hated the whole thing horribly, but one never shows it. The day before my doctor had been taken ill with influenza, and though I asked for another, none could be sent, and there I was with the dead man in the trench and another wounded, and no one to attend to them. However, by dint of sitting up all night, going round the front trenches, etc., I managed to get things more or less right, but was not sorry when day broke without an attack, for if a strong one is made here, we are sure to be broken through. Well, now you would like to hear what sort of place I am in. Imagine a hole in the ground thatched over with mud and broken planks. It is 3 feet deep, and raised just sufficiently for me to sit on the ground without touching my head against the roof. I have some looted straw on the clay, and here I sit and shiver, with my greatcoat and a blanket and mud up to my eyes. From this charming spot I try, with the assistance of many orderlies, to get orders to various companies, sometimes unsuccessfully, for the men lose themselves in a surprising manner when sent on messages. Each time I go forward to the front trenches I have to wade through mud bent double in a little narrow ditch which catches me on either side. We have been told that we are to remain for only forty-eight hours in this place, but it may turn out to be a fortnight for all I know! At present I am using a couple of batteries against the trenches that the Germans are working in on my right. A few men are firing at us from these, but we have hardly fired a shot ourselves, as we are waiting for the enemy to advance, if so inclined. A tremendous bombardment goes on about 10 miles east of us, the heaviest I have heard yet. I nearly went to sleep over this letter, so will stop now, and write more when I have time....

In Trenches.
February 18th, 1915.

You ask about H—— having a pony; I think he had better get thorough confidence in the donkey first, and learn to go by himself. The reason is plain to anyone who goes in for horses much. A donkey, though it kicks a good deal, generally has its hind feet unshod, and in any case does not kick hard enough to more than hurt a little. A pony, on the contrary, is very liable to throw one off and then kick one's skull in. I remember my brother H—— being knocked off and kicked by a mare. A little nearer, and he would never have moved again. Therefore I think it would be wiser to get our boy used to his donkey and not afraid of it. I will have a look at him when (and if) I get home again. Yesterday I went in the afternoon to put our cemetery straight. It was being shelled at the time, and as I crept round some of our batteries afterwards, the guns were being hit, also a rather nice farm in which they were placed surrounded by a moat. The enemy have been shelling us this morning too, very closely, but I am tired, and my nerves, as you know, are not very jumpy! I was up just after 3 o'clock this morning, and went to various places, nearly being lost in a quagmire! Two of my men were hit, one by a spent bullet in the stomach. We can see the bullet, so I expect he will not die. The other was shot through the thigh, and the bullet stuck in his hand! We have got it out, and I am forwarding it to the authorities, as it has taken such a queer shape that one wonders if the German bullets are according to rules. This is a sketch of the bullet as it was originally and now. You can imagine what pain such a thing must give....

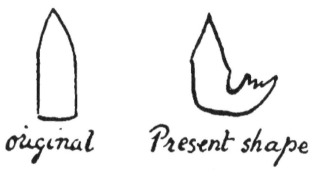

In Billets.
February 19th, 1915.

We are in support now. As we moved down here one of my men was hit in the "hinder parts." Very unfair advantage for an enemy to take. Of course it was dark; we found, however, that he was not dangerously wounded. That man whose bullet I drew you yesterday had his thigh bone smashed, poor fellow! Did you see that some officers who were prisoners had been exchanged by Germany (the incurable ones)? The two seniors mentioned I knew. One was Major Davey of the Middlesex Regt., whose brother lives in Newark. The other is Major Chichester, with whom I used to hunt in Dover. Did you see French's last despatches? I heard from Aden last night. The Colonel next junior to me out there sent all the news. They have had heavy rain, and the whole place is green (?). It is said not to have happened since the Flood! Then I received a pessimistic letter from Aunt H—— telling me that lots of wounded were expected and that the war would not cease. The Kaiser is not running this world's course. He is only allowed to go on as far as is good for him and for us. If he were, I should be pessimistic too, but I have yet to learn that "the arm of the Lord is shortened," and until then we can rest in peace no matter what happens, my dear. I enclose you a cutting from the *People* sent by Aunt H—— about the Saddlers' Co. All the Lauries belong to it. My Father was Master more than once, and also Uncle Alfred. A bright beautiful springlike day, but a little cold. The pudding arrived yesterday; many thanks for it. Our dinner also consisted of smoked sprats from Major Baker; cake and tinned peaches from Capt. Wright; figs and ginger from Mr. Brown, so we did not do badly. We had an adventure last night with a wagon which contained our little all. The man drove carelessly, and the wagon fell into a ditch 3 feet deep in water. After carefully unloading it, I gave them a pair of horses and 50 men to get it out. They pulled it up all right, but it next fell into the ditch on the other side, where it had to be left till the morning, when we sent out just at dawn and brought it in. All this kept us late for dinner, as you may imagine....

In Billets.
February 20th, 1915.

No letters at all, as, owing to the submarines, we are dodging the mails across somewhere else, I expect. The great difficulty is to catch your submarine, though you may see him often enough. The craze for going boating in these vessels will shortly die out amongst the Germans, I fancy, when they find out the number of boats that do not come home! At present they are looking out for one or two which I understand will not reappear, and thus they have to keep ships cruising about in search of them with petrol and food. Of course these are neutral ships; but it adds to our chance of finding out where and how these knaves draw their supplies! I have heard that it is from Ireland; but I expect the Government knows more than it lets out. Yesterday the Germans shelled us for an hour and a half; they just missed us, and killed a poor civilian behind the houses instead. They have increased our leave by one day now; still, whether they will grant mine a second time is uncertain, but I continue to hope. The awkward part is that they never let me know in time to write and tell you. Supposing it is granted, I may arrive on the night of February 25th; but if I do get across I must do a little shopping in London first, and fit myself out with some things I badly want: then I shall come on to you as soon as possible. It is rather a bore that the war will not stop, and I am annoyed that I have been kept out in India and away from you for over two years! The weather is improving here and getting more springlike. What are the Germans going to do now?...

February 21st, 1915.

I was very glad to hear from you yesterday, when two of your letters arrived together. Of course we had been done by these German submarines; so evidently the authorities thought it wiser not to run the Folkestone boats all through the day, for fear of giving the Germans an opportunity of sinking them! I fancy at night you are as likely as not to run over a submarine. In the same way I make no doubt that many of the German ones have been run down and sunk on the quiet. We go into the trenches again to-night, worse luck! My leave was refused on the ground that the General was not giving anyone a second leave, but the Staff captain added that it was only a matter of a few weeks' delay, when he would probably grant it if he could. I have been over to my transport lines on horseback this morning. I have to keep my eye on some 60 horses and mules who mostly stand out in muddy fields; but as they are very well fed and not overworked at present, there is nothing much wrong with them, excepting that their thick woolly coats gather vermin a little. I have had broken bricks and cinders put down for them to stand on, and thus lifted them out of the mud. I was over yesterday getting my hair cut, when I met Mr. Sherlock out for a walk, and as I was obliged to wait for an hour or so, I had tea with him. He told me that my name was mentioned in French's despatches. Well, that is quite pleasant, and I hope next time some of my officers will join me. Do you remember a Col. Gough in Dublin about the time we were married? Well, he is Brigadier-General on the Staff now, and yesterday went down to our lines of trenches. He was shot through the groin, and I am afraid has been very badly wounded. The enemy proceeded to shell E—— yesterday whilst I was there. Their gun must have been 5 miles from it. The first shot knocked a big tree down in a timber yard, of all places, but did no further damage. The second one went over my head, fell in a soft place, and exploded its energy in nothing. Then I left E——. Monson, my old servant, has joined me, looking more like a cross between an owl and a stork than ever!...

In Trenches.
February 23rd, 1915.

Just now we are undergoing a shelling from a heavy German howitzer; a piece fell at my feet as I was outside talking to Col. Spedding, cousin to Major Spedding of my regiment, whom you knew. He tells me that Major S. is supposed to be dead, but the difficulty is that every now and then some rumour comes that he has been seen alive, and poor Mrs. Spedding catches at any hope. He was a brave man, which, after all, is what we want.

I enclose you my sister Amy's letter. Yesterday I had to go off to look at some forts. The German snipers were busy, though there was so thick a mist that they could not see me. Still, their bullets fell pretty close, and hit one of the forts; a man was also wounded in the leg. It shows how dangerous this unaimed fire can be when it comes in quantities. I had a quaint postcard from Sydney in reply to my last letter. Yes; I saw that Massereene, poor Herbert Stepney, and many others I know were mentioned in the despatches. The Military Cross is a new order, awarded to junior officers. As to the Russians, they have large numbers of men, but are still unfortunately short of equipment. Germany had plenty of men, though she never imagined that she would have to get the last 2 millions out. They were not trained, but neither were the Russians; I think, however, that we shall wear them down all right in the end. The Germans are supposed to have used up half their last million already. Our days here are very hard; for instance, I was up at 2 a.m., and have been walking or working ever since then, arranging with engineers or Generals or artillery officers what is to be done. I lay down for an hour after 6 o'clock, but could not sleep on account of cold feet.

In Trenches.
February 24rd, 1915.

I am glad you had a pleasant "meet" at Ossington, and I am much obliged for Mr. Denison's kind inquiries after me. I know how seriously ill he is, but I think it is quite likely many of us will go before.... We had a sharp frost last night, though my men are fairly used to it now. They are just like a lot of naughty children! For instance, I had two killed yesterday, through either their own or their comrades' faults. One man was watching our guns shelling the enemy's trenches. He was told to lie down or he would be shot. He did so, and the moment he saw a favourable opportunity he popped up again, and was promptly shot dead. The other was in front of the trenches mending wires, and his comrades, seeing that their N.C. officer was out, joyfully seized the occasion to stoke their fire and have a big blaze. The result was the unfortunate man showed up against it and was shot through the head; and their fire was kicked bodily into the water by an irate N.C.O. But they will do exactly the same to-morrow and the next day and the day after! The fact is, they never think! I am waiting now to take the Brigade Major and one of "K.'s Army" round the trenches to show them what I can, so that K.'s officer may not have quite a "green" crew when he arrives. More Germans have gathered in front of us lately, I think. I have written to London for an awfully good new waterproof, as I must keep dry, and I have had to send to "Flight" for a new uniform coat. When they come I shall be fairly set up, though the trenches have played havoc with my riding things; but they will have to do for the present. Would you kindly look in my unpainted tin-lined box and get me out a pair of khaki puttees. If you cannot find them there, they will be in a black wooden box. Get someone to help you. Both trunks are in the box-room, but do not catch cold when watching them. I have now returned from the trenches. We were sniped a little; the General went up another trench alongside us with the adjutant of a certain regiment, Capt. Thompson, and he, poor fellow! was killed. He was a good sort, and was in here yesterday to see me, and talking about his 3 children so cheerily: one, a boy, at, I think, the Beacon School, Sevenoaks, and on his way to Eton. Mr. Adderley came back this morning with a wonderful story that the Navy had caught an oil tank vessel supplying oil to the German submarines, and that the crew were taken to our Depot in Belfast and there shot! Presumably it is not true!...

February 25th, 1915.

Thanks for your letter. I heard from Sir John, and there was one, too, from my Mother, who is a very regular correspondent. Aunt Mary Cowell's letter turned up also, so I must get letters of thanks written to everyone in due course. To-night I am dining with Gen. Pinney. He and I are supposed to be the two optimists of the Division. Snow on the ground and rather cold. I hope the Germans are very cold and short of food! I am waiting to find out the time of poor Capt. Thompson's funeral. He was killed when with the General yesterday, as I told you. Sir John Ross is most kind in his remarks, is he not? I thought I had told you that B. and M.'s matches duly arrived. I am sure, in fact, that I did do so. Hal is not too young to ride a pony soon, though Sydney would be; but then you want a man to keep him well on the lead at first. My idea is, as I said before, that when he gets absolutely *au fait* with his donkey, it would be time enough to put him on a pony. When a boy is over 8 or 9, it is safe to let him ride regularly. Earlier than that, I don't approve of. I fancy that this Dardanelles business, if properly run, will lead to great results. Personally, I always thought that they had too many troops in Egypt for the sole purpose of defence. Now I suppose they will put some of them up the Dardanelles, and Dame Rumour says that Generals of the Naval Divisions have gone across to the Dardanelles already, but, of course, that may not be true....

(*From Sir J. Ross of Bladensburg.*)

Rostrevor House,
Rostrevor, Ireland.
20.2.15.

My dear G———,

Very many congratulations on your being mentioned in despatches, which we are so delighted to see. All the more credit to you that, although you have been out at the front for some time, you were not there at the beginning of the war, and I know in all these cases, when other things are equal, the "mention" goes to those who have been out the longest. I think you know about as much of what is going on as we do, for, on the whole, we are told very little. Yet I am glad to say we are promised two short official accounts every week, and so we must be grateful for that amount of news. The main question outside the actual operations relates to the German intention; if they can torpedo every ship they see, whether it belongs to a belligerent or a neutral! It was always held to be a piece of cruel barbarity to sink a trading vessel without notice, even if belonging to a belligerent nation, the right course being to find out first whether she is a belligerent or not, and then to capture her. It was never considered fair warfare to touch a neutral. But who can say what "Kultur" will bring us to? Most people would call it unblushing piracy and attempted wholesale murder. But we will see what happens. Naval "Kultur" began the day before yesterday, and the report to-day is that a Norwegian neutral was torpedoed. F——— is very well, but does not come here till April. Sydney is here, and is getting fat and chubby, a delightful little boy, and keeps us all very cheery. We have had two delicious days as far as weather is concerned. I hope you have had the same change for the better.

May God keep you safe and sound, dear old G———, is, with our love, our very earnest hope.

I am,
Yours affectionately,
J.R. of B———.

February 26th, 1915.

We went to poor Capt. Thompson's funeral yesterday, Major B. and myself. A military funeral in the field is of three sorts. Well away from the enemy the soldier is borne on a stretcher, sewn up in his blankets and wrapped in a flag. Nearer the enemy you dispense with a flag; and finally, of course, in the trenches, when you cannot get out, you crawl down a ditch and dig a hole in the side and bury the poor fellow. Ours was of the second sort, as it was within long-range rifle fire, but somewhat screened by a hedge. Four officers carried the stretcher, and about six others followed behind. The grave was lined with wheaten straw, unthreshed, and the clergyman read a very short service, and then we all slipped quietly away. After the funeral we trotted on to the 5th Battery. They are friends of ours, and had been heavily shelled the day before; we telephoned them to inquire the result, but had received no answer. The operator, it seems, was obliged to take refuge in a cellar with some women and children, for the enemy positively rained shells upon them, fortunately, however, from a field gun only. Then shells struck the house itself, and the others made holes in the ground round it. Two went through the adjoining windows, two others into the dust-heap, etc. The cause of it was that the French owner had brought a threshing machine and was threshing out his wheat. Of course, the smoke of the engine attracted the Germans at once. The French are very much amused at this, I am told, for they do not allow any such things near their lines; but our Staff are soft-hearted. I had a very pleasant little dinner with Gen. Pinney last night, and played Bridge for an hour—the first game I have had time for since I left the transport at Liverpool. That will give you an idea of how busy I am. When I can, I sleep; otherwise I work hard. We are looking forward to more tartlets. I do not believe in riding lessons at present for H——. Let Sheppard teach him. My father showed me how to hold the reins, and I learnt the remainder myself. Far and away the best way too....

February 27th, 1915.

A very cold day with east wind. It will be bitter in the trenches. I hope the Germans are finding it so! I send you a note from some R.I.C. Sergeant in Belfast. Your extract from the Irish *Evening Telegraph* about me is rather amusing! As to your going to Ireland, it is early yet to decide. Who knows what a day may bring forth at any time? So poor Mr. Gorton has gone. The people in his village will miss him greatly. I will try and put a note in this letter for Patience Gorton, as I know her best, and you can send it on. I always forget the name of their place. By the way, I remember now that it is called Walesby, so will post it direct and save you the trouble. I am glad you thought of sending a wreath. I went for a long ride with the object of seeing someone in the Border Regt. yesterday whom Major Baker knew. Not one officer who came out with that regiment is with it now. This gives you an idea of what is going on here....

ROYAL IRISH CONSTABULARY BARRACKS,
Chichester Park, Belfast.
February 20th, 1915.

Lieutenant-Colonel G.B. Laurie.

Sir,

We write to say how very glad we are to see that you are safe and well. We were delighted to see by the papers that you were among those mentioned for gallantry in the despatch sent home a few days ago by Field-Marshal Sir John French. We have tried to locate the different gentlemen now on active service who had been residing in this district, and the press is our medium—it was there we learnt you were at the front, and we are most anxious, and dearly hope that they all, who were when here so very kind to us, and are now risking their lives that we may be free—may be restored to their homes in perfect health and strength.

This is the spirit which prompts the writing of this letter, and we beg of you not to think us unduly familiar, but rather that we most sincerely hope that you may have perfect health and strength, and, above all, that you may, when the time comes, return home safe and well.

Your obedient servant,
JEREMIAH LEE,
Sergt. R.I.C.

February 28th, 1915.

I had a hurried ride yesterday in a piercing wind to see my 70 or 80 horses. In the afternoon, just as we were starting off to the trenches, we were stopped and told to wait whilst the Gunners tried to cut the wire in front of the German trenches with shells. Such a course of action may lead to heavy sniping, as you can quite well imagine. However, we got in all right by eight o'clock, and I wandered round my trenches until between 12 and 1 o'clock a.m. This morning we received a notice that we were to be withdrawn to reserve to-morrow or the next day, owing to more troops coming into the line. I had to take the General round who succeeds me in these trenches. He seemed such a nice man. We are supposed to leave to-morrow night if these people can get out from their trenches. The enemy is shelling us now, and as it is a particularly clear day they are using it to the best advantage to try and destroy us. I must turn our guns on to them if they go on like this. I only wish we could swamp the brutes with numbers and get the war over. I am not disturbed about Russia. If we can get the Dardanelles open, we can easily send her ammunition and equipment for her spare men, and so end the war more quickly; but, failing that, I think Russia will easily foil Germany, and spring at her again and again until she is worn out. I had a letter of congratulation from your sister Mabel. Very kind of her....

In Trenches.
Ash Wednesday, 1915.

A wet, muggy morning. I have been waiting for 3 hours to accompany the General round the lines since 6.30 a.m. At 9.30 I telephoned in, and found that he had gone to some other duty and forgotten me! However, it cannot be helped. He and I are really very friendly. More fighting on our right, with very heavy big gun fire. I expect the brickfields at La Bassée are again being a scene of mortal combat. We were ordered last night to try to ascertain if the Germans still occupied their trenches as usual; so we crept out and looked about, and found everything much the same. As to the khaki-coloured shirts, would you have them put away by sizes, please, when they are made up, till wanted; the present ones will wear out with a rush from being worn night and day, and from having been badly washed and scorched when drying, so they may be wanted in a hurry. Whilst waiting about here this morning, I amused myself by looking for shell holes round our ruins. So far as I can see, they are everywhere, like the holes in a sponge for numbers. My artillery is just going to blow up a house where the enemy hid a machine gun last night, and which opened on us during the night and thought we did not know! I also have another R.A. officer throwing tins full of gun cotton and nails into the German trenches at this very moment. A nice Christian occupation, truly! I ought to know in a few days if there is any chance of second leave or not.

LETTERS OF MARCH, 1915.

In Trenches.
March 1st, 1915.

I enclose you a letter from one of my old Generals, Sir John Keir. I wrote to congratulate him on receiving the "K" to his C.B., which I helped to win him at Boshbult, S. Africa, 1902. Do not trouble to send it back again. They have no children, and I have never met Lady Keir so far, but if I get back to England no doubt I shall, though his division is in Cork at present. Yesterday we were once more under heavy fire. One shell exploded beside two men who were trying to make some tea. I am sure the poor fellows, without thinking, gave away their position by having too large a fire. Anyway, this shell burnt everything round them, including the flaps of a barn door standing upright, with nothing inflammable near, but the doors were in a blaze in a moment, and also their clothes. One man had 18 holes in him; the other was dreadfully scorched and hurt. I gave him morphia tablets, but I'm afraid they did not do him much good; it was a mercy that the doctor arrived soon to give him a proper hypodermic injection. In one place we found a piece of shell about the size of a half lb. iron weight which had forced its way right through, and was just under the skin on the other side. We got that out, but he died shortly after. They shelled us again during the night, the brutes; however, we did not bother our heads much about that, and I had a very good night's rest from 10 o'clock until four a.m. After all, it was not G—— S——'s husband that I met the other day. He turned out to be Capt. Sherlock of a Militia Artillery regt., one of the family, I fancy, who was tea-planting or something at Singapore before the war. As to smoked herrings, I cannot say that I am very fond of them, so I think that at present it would be as well not to send anything but cakes, mincepies, or tartlets. Mincepies are presumably over, so continue to send jam tartlets, please. Some day I will try to get our cook here to see what he can do, but I am afraid our soldier man needs more instruction before he can venture on pastry! Now I must stop, as I have a great deal of other business to get done....

They have started shelling us again, bless them!

March 3rd, 1915.

I was so busy yesterday that I had not a chance of sending you more than a postcard. They sent for me to a hurried conference of the General. I then rode off with another Colonel some miles, and after putting on waders had to reconnoitre our new trenches and go over other ground, marching along these under fire, with the mud, as usual, halfway up to my waist. Such is life over here. I returned about 3 o'clock, and then I had to settle the endless questions which arise in a regt. on active service, from getting the men new boots to arranging whether it was safe for the shoemaker to have a fire in his corner whilst he was busy cobbling. So far the tarts have not arrived. Perhaps they will presently. All the war news looks good; but it is a big war. I only wish I had been out with the "Rufford" at Weston last week. Such a horrible day here, raining hard and everything uncomfortable. I have managed to squeeze into a small house with my adjutant Capt. Wright, and he has to sleep on the boards where we have our meals, whilst the old lady and her servant cook our rations at 1-½ francs a day each. You should hear the French we talk!...

Glad the children liked the "meet."

March 4th, 1915.

Your letter did not turn up yesterday! I have been most busy with various things. If you saw my men in a spinning mill sleeping under engines, etc., you would wonder how we exist! Of course, Spring is coming on, and we shall then have to go in for business of the worst type; so whilst someone else is holding the lines, we are now trying to get our men fit for this work. Meals here are quaint, run by a servant girl. She brings breakfast of coffee without milk and an omelette, but we always have our ration of bacon as well. That was a difficulty at first, as neither the adjutant's nor my book gave the French for bacon. However, by introducing the word *cochon*, we arrived at the fact that here amongst her class it was called *porc*—so there we are! Then luncheon is a sad affair, with generally some cold thing followed only by cheese. At tea (made very weak) from our ration stuff, she now gives us toast, though there, again, we had no such word in our book. I managed to remember that it was *pain roti*, and we got along. Dinner is not bright, but yesterday we were blessed with a pudding of rice strongly flavoured with vanilla. To-day I am off for a wade with my officers to show them what they must learn about my new lines. Such a trouble as it is getting there, with shell flying and bursting all around one, and rifle bullets humming everywhere. I hate this business cordially, but what will you! If these scamps are not driven back, they will try to rule the world, and will kill and burn as they think fit, and that will not do at all! The Russians seem to be doing good work in killing the unfortunate Germans. Let us hope that the whole thing will go with a run now, and that it will not last much longer.... Love to the children....

P.S.—I lost two N.C.Os. killed yesterday by one bullet through their heads, and another of my poor men had his tongue cut out.

March 5th, 1915.

My dearest F——

I am writing this in great haste, as I am just off to the General's on important business. I was most interested in reading various friends' letters on my "mention." What it has really been in the way of being shot at would cover a small campaign three times over, and I do not doubt many of my officers and men have had even a worse time than myself, and there is very much more hard work to come. The French Army can always produce fresh troops for each fresh job, but our smaller army has to send the same troops up to everything, and then when the regiment is reduced to fragments, it is filled up with anyone from anywhere, and to the authorities it is the same as the original good regiment. Before I forget, and in case anything happens to me, I want to tell you again that all my securities are at Cox; there is a list of them in my despatch case, and you will find one lot of title deeds that I had not as yet had time to look over in the Oak Room. I have been so hustled ever since coming from India that it has been impossible to attend to such things....

Yours with love....
G.B.L.

In Billets.
March 7th, 1915.

We have been very hard at work to-day. At 9.30 last night I received an order to arrange with the priest in a certain village for service the next morning. As my billets extend over a mile, you can imagine that I was not too pleased! This was followed at 11.30 p.m. by another order that we were to be on parade at 6 a.m. Getting home between 7 and 8 a.m., I had to hurry to early service, bolt some breakfast, and present myself at the General's house at 9 o'clock for a conference. Returning from that, I then had to hand in the men's winter kits. Next came the orders to move into fresh billets to-night in the dark. This with 1,000 men and 70 horses, whilst I must send a working party of four hundred men to a place 5 or 6 miles off at 10.30 p.m. to-night. How it is all to be done I have not been informed, but you can imagine the chaos that can ensue. We have been comfortable for the last two or three days. After our life in the trenches we can say that we have been *very* comfortable, because we have been able to wash daily and have a tub every second day, which things count much. I sent my Sam Browne belt, etc., home two days ago, as we are supposed to wear web equipment now like the men; and our swords have also been despatched. Mine has gone to Messrs. Cox's shipping agency through the Ordnance, with three labels on it addressed to you; it is well greased, and will not require overhauling, I trust, until I get back. We have had two days of rain, and things are rather nasty. My saddle-bags are quite useful on my second horse; they take a lot of my kit, including a pair of waders, with boots to go with them too. When the weather dries up a little, I shall return these and push other things in. I wish the war was well over, but I expect the Germans hate it worse than we do....

BILLETS.
March 8th, 1915.

Our little march in the dark was accompanied with heavy rain squalls and the weather turning bitterly cold. We missed our billeting party in the darkness, for it was intense. I think the inside of a public house was appealing to them at the time, so I halted my men, and by sending mounted officers in every direction, with luck I caught some of them. And here we are again, and very comfortable. Of course, we still have our early rising to contend with, but otherwise for the moment things are pretty straight. These Irishmen are most amusing fellows; they can't be treated like the English soldier: one has to be much more strict with them, and ride them at other times with a much lighter hand. For the next few months, unless Germany collapses at once, there will be *heavy fighting* for us. I am glad to hear that the Russians are driving these knaves back. What it really means is that when the Germans fight a successful action, they lose a certain number of men whom they cannot replace, and use up ammunition which they cannot make in a hurry, and so the war gradually draws to its conclusion, I trust.... I had to fly away just then to deal with my many prisoners and my companies also. I am sorry you have had illness in the house; I am so used to sickness that it hardly appals me when it applies to other people. For instance, since I came out here, if you multiply the number of my Father's town house in Porchester Terrace by 10 [number invalided, 470] you will be below the numbers who have been invalided from my Bn. since I came to France, and before that there was Hursley Park, Winchester, and the voyage home from India, when I lived amongst sick men for some unknown reason. The weather is now varying between skiffs of snow and bright gleams of sunshine, but very, very cold....

March 9th, 1915.

Many thanks for your letter. My new puttees will be most useful, as my old ones are full of holes. We have, during the last day or so, had a strong wind, and the ground is drying up wonderfully, so it will not be so hard on puttees for the future. As a rule, when one walks across country, and struggles through muddy trenches without one's horse, one wears puttees if one is not wearing long gum boots; these latter keep the legs and feet drier, but the difficulty is that they are too heavy to walk very far in them. I had a long letter from Meta, which I enclose. I am sending two badges to the children from my old coat. I thought they might like them. I look forward very much to the cake you are sending, as the last parcel went astray. My new coat came last night. It is made out of very thick cloth, and altogether loose and useful. There always has been a battalion of the London Irish Rifles (Volunteers), now a territorial corps. The War Office would not allow them to belong to us, because Irish Regiments have no territorial Bns. In S. Africa, that Bn. (London Irish Rifles) sent us a company which was attached to our regiment throughout the war. I leave the Irish visit in your hands at present. The only leave I shall receive will be if I am wounded. There will be a lot of fighting of a bad sort from now on. It would never be surprising if one were hit. I have been mercifully preserved up to now; and, again, one must put one's trust in Providence....

My dear little Hal,

I am enclosing one of the coat badges which I wore in S. Africa and in this war until this morning, when I received another coat from my tailor, so I thought you would like it to keep. I hope you are a good boy and working very hard, and are a help to Mummie.

Your affectionate
Daddie.

March 9th, 1915.

My dear little Blanche,

I am also sending you one of my coat badges. This morning I received from my tailor a much warmer coat, I am glad to say, for I find it terribly cold being out all night in mud and ice-cold water. I am sure you are trying to be a very good girl and learning your lessons well.

Your loving
Daddie.

March 9th, 1915.

IN TRENCHES. VERY MUCH!
March 11th, 1915.

I have had some very hard fighting since I wrote to you. Of course I knew it was coming off, but could not tell you exactly.... We lost a certain amount.... I am too busy, though, to write much, and I am out in the open feeling very cold, and will be in the mud all night, where, by the bye, I've been for the past three nights. A few of my officers have been killed, I regret to say, whilst the total of killed and wounded for my regiment alone has been three times the number of my father's house in P—— Terrace [total number, 141]. Can you imagine me charging down with the regiment shortly after dawn into Neuve Chapelle? I will write more about it all if I am spared. There is heavy fighting before us.

Yours ever....
G.B.L.

[Here the letters end abruptly, this being the last one written just after the taking of Neuve Chapelle. On the following day, March 12th, the Irish Rifles were ordered to advance to a further position, which, although the ground was gained, the task was an almost impossible one, the men being completely worn out after fighting hard several days and nights together.

The story of how Colonel Laurie led the charge will be found in the letters appended, with various other descriptions of the battle. Cheering on his men and calling to them to follow him, he fell in action mortally wounded. Thus was he summoned in a moment to a higher life, and his pilgrimage on earth was over].

R.I.P.

Buckingham Palace, O.H.M.S.

To Mrs. Laurie, Carlton Hall, Carlton-on-Trent, Notts.

The King and Queen deeply regret the loss you and the Army have sustained by the death of your husband in the service of his country. Their Majesties truly sympathize with you in your sorrow.

Private Secretary.

(*From Major Clinton Baker, Second-in-Command.*)

R.I. Rifles.
14/3/15.

Dear Mrs. Laurie,

You will have received your dreadful news by telegram. I cannot tell you what a terrible loss it has been to the whole regiment, whose deepest sympathy you have. Our dear Colonel was killed on March 12th at 5.30 p.m. as he rose to lead a charge, revolver in hand—a fine example to us all. The end was instantaneous, no suffering.

His adjutant early next morning, out with me, was shot dead at my side, and we last evening after dark buried them side by side close to Neuve Chapelle. We had three terrific days' fighting (10th, 11th, 12th), and are still engaged. I will answer any questions you may ask as soon as I can. I am writing this in the position we captured, knowing that you must be longing for even a short letter. I cannot tell you what a *loss* I have suffered. You have my very deepest sympathy.

Yours most sincerely,
W. Clinton Baker.

Everything will be sent home in due course.

(*From the same.*)

24/3/15.

I am glad to think that my hurried note was of some little comfort to you. It was written practically during the battle, so you must excuse its apparent briefness. My poor Colonel was absolutely without fear, a splendid example, which I am glad to say the men well followed. The grave is within two hundred yards of the German trenches and 50 yards from where he fell. It is now marked with the rough cross we put up, with his name on it, but I am getting a substantial one erected similar to those he had put up for all the regiment who have fallen during the last four months.

As he no doubt told you, we attended the Holy Communion together only five days before he fell.... I will have "Peace, perfect Peace" put on the cross. His sword was sent off to Cox and Co. about the 5th, and they will send it to you, together with all his other effects which have been sent off. But you should write to them.

I cannot tell you how I miss him; we were so much together every day and every night. Don't hesitate to write to ask me questions.

The first part of the fight I think he wrote and told you about; I know he said he was engaged in writing to you, on the 11th I think it was. The 10th was the day on which we stormed the trenches and took Neuve Chapelle. On the 11th we did little except get shelled, as we tried to sleep in some German trenches. On the morning of the 12th we were again in Neuve Chapelle, and for 2-½ hours endured a terrific shelling to which he paid no heed, and, as I told you, the fatal shot came at 5.20 p.m. just as, revolver in hand, I saw him about to get over our parapet and lead a charge. A true soldier's Death. Should I write to his Mother? I would rather not if you can do so, but will, of course, if you wish it. I am so sorry for you and for your poor children.

Yours very sincerely,
W. Clinton Baker.

(From the same.)

1. R.I. Rifles.
12/4/15.

I am afraid I have been a very long time answering your letter of March 30th.

I hope you will be able to get a photograph of the grave, as Capt. Jeffares of our fourth Battalion, now attached to the 2nd Munster Fusiliers, who knew the Colonel well, writes that he has taken a photograph of it and will send you one. There will probably be only a rough cross on the grave, which we put up on the day he was buried. Capt. Jeffares wrote that he had tidied up round the grave.

One of our men soon after the fight wrote home as follows:—"Our Colonel and Adjutant lie side by side guarding the ground won till the last Trump!"

We have now lost Capt. Lanyon, very sad, so soon after Capt. Biscoe being killed. They had been inseparable friends for years.

                                                    Yours sincerely,
                                                    W. Clinton Baker.

(From Brigadier-General Oldfield (at this time Major R.F.A., attached Royal Irish Rifles) to Hon. Lady Ross of Bladensburg.)

                                                    On F.S.
                                                    18/3/15.

Dear Aunt B——,

I am writing to tell you how Col. Laurie fell. I was talking to him just before his charge, and you will perhaps tell or not tell Mrs. Laurie what I write as you think fit. Part I saw and part I was told of after. On the 11th afternoon, after taking Neuve Chapelle, our Infantry was brought to a standstill, and the experiment was tried of rushing a field gun up to clear away houses, obstacles, etc., in the open. I was chosen for this task. After helping our Infantry in one place on 12th morning, I was told to help the R.I. Rifles to take some houses and a trench in the evening. I rushed over to arrange with him, and went into his trenches and among his men. All were very exhausted. He said they simply could not go on. We arranged to attack in the morning. I went to the Brigadier to say so, but found that he was ordered to attack at once. Col. Laurie knew it was almost impossible, but ran off to obey. I rushed to my gun. I just had time to blow in a barn before the time of attack came. His men tried again and again—only to be mown down. The ground between the two lines of trenches was thick with dead of both sides. Colonel Laurie said, "Follow me, I will lead you!" rushed out, and fell gallantly, shot dead at the head of his men. Is there a finer death? For myself, I escaped with my guns last night, and here I am resting after a desperate 9 days. But I lost my favourite subaltern and nearly every friend I had in the Division. I am still very lame, and this time has been very strenuous.

                                                    Your affec. nephew,
                                                    L. Oldfield.

(From Colonel Laurie's Brigadier.[10]*)*

                                                    March 23rd.

Dear Mrs. Laurie,

You will have heard by now the sad news of your husband's death, and it is but cold comfort to offer you my sincerest sympathy. It will, however, be a satisfaction to you to hear how well he was thought of. He commanded his Battalion with distinction, and, I hoped, would have lived to have risen higher. He died a soldier's death, gallantly leading his men in the face of the enemy; and his memory will live among the gallant men who have done so much to keep the fine traditions of the British Army unsullied. He is buried with his brother officers near where he fell. If I can help you in any way, I hope you will not scruple to tell me. My wife will also have written to you, and is very anxious to hear if she can do anything for you.

Yours very truly,
A. Lowry Cole.

(From Lieutenant-Colonel Percy Laurie, D.S.O.)

Headquarters,
3rd Cav. Div.,
Expeditionary Force.
March, 1915.

My Dear F——,

My heart's right there with you. There is little doubt how he died, gallantly cheering on his men; the whole thing has made history. I will go over and get the fullest particulars, find his grave, have it carefully marked, and send you a photo. He would wish you to be like himself, brave and trusting in the future.

Let me know if I can do anything....

(From the same, later.)

I went over to-day to make inquiries and find George's grave. I went to his regiment and found a brother officer who was with him when he was killed. A bullet struck him to the right of the nose and killed him instantaneously; he was about to lead his regiment to the charge. His servant stayed with him, but has not been seen since; it is thought he has been hit by a shell. George is buried by the side of his adjutant in a little garden in the village, between two houses on the west side. The grass is marked by a cross, and is fenced round. I know the exact spot. 9 officers were killed, 9 wounded, 400 men killed and wounded. So the gallant old fellow rests with most of his officers and men. His personal effects have been collected and sent to you.

Everyone was loud in their praise of him, and the General said he had lost a gallant officer. I could not reach the grave to-day, as it was not safe. I was nearly shot as it was! I got to within 200 yards. Let me know if I can do anything else for you. God bless you!

Percy.

"AFTERWARDS."

A FEW OTHER LETTERS, EXTRACTS, ETC., RECEIVED IN 1915.

(The words of a brother officer—Major Cooke Collis, Brigade Major, 31st Brigade.)

1915.

... I hope Colonel Laurie did not suffer. It must help you to bear your sorrow to know that he died as he would have wished, fighting bravely for his country. I feel his death keenly; we were so much together in the old days, and now, how the regiment is changed, and how dreadfully they have suffered! But the name they have won for History will not easily be forgotten....

(Extract from a letter written by Rifleman Patrick White, "D" Coy., 1st Battalion Royal Irish Rifles.)

... Yes, it was our Battalion that Colonel G.B. Laurie commanded. I was about two yards from him when he was killed. Before I tell you how he came to be killed, I must tell you how sorry we all were. He was the best Colonel we ever had, he was always merry and bright, and had a smile for both his men and officers; he was a hero, as General French told us.

On the morning of March 9th he (Colonel Laurie) told us that we had to make a charge at a place called Neuve Chapelle. We were marched to the firing line that night, and our Colonel had a very nice meal ready for us before we went into the trenches.

About 7.30 the next morning there began the biggest bombardment I have ever heard—our big guns roared out. I thought hell had been let loose. I tried to look before me, but could see nothing but flame and smoke, and the roars of the big guns were terrible. In about an hour's time our Colonel gave us the word to fix bayonets and charge for the German trenches. He led us with a smile, and gained victory for our Battalion that day. During the whole time he took it nice and cool, and kept us all in good spirits. The following morning our Battalion was to make another advance, and it was in this advance we lost our brave and noble hero. When a platoon went over the parapet, some of our boys fell never to rise again, and our Colonel, seeing this, was looking over the parapet. There was an enfilading fire from the right, and we told the Colonel to keep his head down; but he was not thinking of himself, but of his men lying out there.

Just then he was hit—shot through the head. We bandaged him up, but it was no good. Our brave Colonel had departed from us, and we can only hope that he has got his reward for his heroism in the next world....

(From 4872 Corporal J. Lennon, "A" Coy., 3rd Royal Irish Rifles, Victoria Barracks, Belfast.)

1915.

Dear Madam,

I now take the opportunity of writing to you as regards the death of your late husband, Colonel G.B. Laurie, who was O.C. of the 1st Bn. Royal Irish Rifles. He was my Commanding Officer for nearly two years. I followed him on the morning of March 10th, 1915, when the Battle of Neuve Chapelle was taking place. He was the first man who charged into Neuve Chapelle. I was present with him all through the battle, and I was with him when he met his death on March 12th just at 20 mins. to 5 o'clock, when he was about to lead the charge of his battalion. His death was instantaneous, and he was buried on March 13th: it was I who carried him in after he was wounded, and when I found that he was quite dead I said some prayers over his body. Major Wright was also wounded in the same battle. I was very sorry indeed about the death of my Commanding Officer. He was a soldier and a gentleman, fearless in all his actions and honest, just and upright. I will certainly never forget him for his kindness to me and all the men who fought under him.

I was mentioned in Sir J. French's Despatch along with my Commanding Officer, Colonel Laurie, for bravery at the Battle of Neuve Chapelle. You will find my name in the list. I regret his death very much; it was a great blow to me. Well, Madam, the only thing I have to say before concluding is that his relatives and friends may well be proud of him, because he was one of the bravest men that ever led men. I would very much like to have a photo of our Colonel, and I remain,

Your obedient servant,
J. Lennon.

(From Earl Manvers.)

Thoresby Park,
Ollerton, Notts.
March 19th, 1915.

Dear Mrs. Laurie,

I feel that I must send one line to say how deeply grieved I was to hear your husband had been killed at the front. I knew him as a most excellent sportsman, and mourn his loss very much. My deep sympathy is with you at this sad time when your home is made desolate.

Please do not think of answering this.

I remain,
Yours sincerely,
Manvers.

(From Brigadier-General Farmar, C.B., C.M.G.)

Headquarters, 2nd Army.
March 20th, 1915.

My dear Mrs. Laurie,

I cannot tell you how shocked I was to hear the dreadful news: only to-night; but you at home must have heard of it days ago. B———'s letter was my first intimation. Somehow it came absolutely unexpectedly: of course, one lives in the middle of these awful sights and happenings, but he was so strong and so full of energy that it seemed unbelievable that he should be taken. He has been a friend of mine, and a very real one, for a good many years now. I saw him not long ago. He would have been sure to have got a Brigade soon if this terrible thing had not happened. I have heard no details, but will try and find out and tell you: unfortunately, his battalion is right at the other end of the line to where we are, but if I can get down I will. Dear Mrs. Laurie, I do feel for you most deeply, and my own loss of a friend as well. If there is anything I can do, it would be a kindness to ask me, and a relief to do something for you.

Yours very sincerely,
Jaspar Farmar.

(From Colonel Anderson.)

Headquarters, 8th Division.
March 22nd, 1915.

Dear Mrs. Laurie,

About ten days ago I received a copy of Col. Laurie's "History of the Royal Irish Rifles" which he had very kindly promised to send me. I was kept very busy on duty, so much so that I never had time to see him and thank him. And now, to my great grief, I have to write and tell you how very grateful I was for the book, and at the same time how very deeply I sympathize with you in your great loss. I need scarcely tell you how splendidly the Royal Irish Rifles did in the battle of Neuve Chapelle, and how grandly they were led by their Colonel.

My father had been in the 83rd many years ago, and I had written the history of my own regiment, so we had bonds of sympathy, and I had had several talks with your husband. So you must please accept my very deepest sympathy in his death, and in your very great loss.

Believe me,
Yours sincerely,
W. Hasturp Anderson.

(*From a cousin.*)

Antrim Castle,
Ireland.
March 24th, 1915.

... I had the very greatest respect for George; he was an ideal soldier and comrade. May God in His mercy comfort you!...

Massereene.

(*From Mrs. Clinton Baker.*)

Bayfordbury,
Hertford.
March 28th, 1915.

Writing of her son, she says: "Osbert feels his Colonel's death deeply. When telling me of it, he said: 'I *could* only write a short letter; I know you will have written to Mrs. Laurie to try to soften the blow.'—'Ten young officers and 250 men have now been sent out from home.'"

(*From General and Mrs. Bird.*[11])

22, Albany Villas,
Brighton.
March 29th, 1915.

... We have not written to tell you how deeply we sympathize with you in your great sorrow, as I know letters are of no comfort in times of sadness, but to-day, in a letter we received, such words of admiration were written of Colonel Laurie that I felt I should like to write and repeat them: "Colonel Laurie handled his battalion to perfection during the attack on Neuve Chapelle, and his death is an irreparable loss to the 1st Battalion."

We have always heard what a splendid soldier Colonel Laurie was, and our country does so need such leaders now in the army to bring victory....

(From General Sir John Keir, K.C.B.)

May 4th, 1915.

Dear Mrs. Laurie,

I have such a deep admiration and respect for your late husband, for Col. Laurie was, as you know, in command of the 28th M.I. in the column I commanded in S. Africa, where I learnt to appreciate his value as a soldier and his many other sterling qualities. After the campaign we used to hear from one another on occasions of mutual congratulation and the like. His loss to the Service is a very great one, but one cannot imagine a more glorious ending to a fine career, falling at the head of the regiment he loved so well, and which he led with such skill and bravery. His name remains one held in honour for all time.

Yours sincerely,
J.N. Keir.

(From General the Right Hon. Sir Nevil Macready, G.C.M.G., K.C.B.)

War Office.
April 2nd, 1915.

My dear Mrs. Laurie,

Only yesterday I was aware of your address. I write only a line to ask you to accept my deep and sincere sympathy in the loss you have sustained. You indeed have given to the Country of your best, and if there is any consolation it may be in the fact that my old friend died as every soldier would wish to, at the head of his battalion in a successful action.

Trusting you and the children are well.

Yours ever sincerely,
C.N. Macready.

(From W.F.E. Denison, Esq.)[12]

Ossington,
Newark, Notts.
July 18th, 1915.

Dear Mrs. Laurie,

Thank you so much for sending me that nice photograph of Colonel Laurie. I think the likeness is excellent. I am so glad to possess it, and shall value it greatly always. I do think of him so constantly, every time I go by Carlton and see all the things there in which he took so great an interest, and the fields where one went shooting, and he was so keen about it all. There is a recollection for me at almost every gateway. He was indeed a most kind and sympathetic neighbour to us and a real friend. Thank you again and again for the photograph; it is most kind of you to have sent it to me.

Yours very sincerely,
W.F.E. Denison.

Lady Cicely Pierrepont wrote:—

Thoresby Park,
Ollerton, Notts.
September 15th, 1915.

Dear Mrs. Laurie,

... I have never had the opportunity till now of telling you how we all felt Colonel Laurie's death, nor how much his unfailing cheery and cheering presence in the hunting field has been and will again be missed by all who had the pleasure of knowing him, and everybody who hunted with him will always retain the very pleasantest memories of his kindness....

The following is an extract from 4th Corps Orders, dated March 14th, 1915, by Lieutenant-General Sir Henry Rawlinson, Bart., K.C.B., C.V.O.:—

"The brilliant success which the troops of the 4th Corps have achieved in the capture of Neuve Chapelle is of the first importance to the Allied cause, especially at this period of the war. The heroism and gallantry of the regimental Officers and men, and the assistance afforded them by the artillery units, is deserving of the highest praise, and the Corps Commander desires to congratulate them on the severe defeat they have inflicted on the enemy, whose losses amount to not less than 4,000 men in killed and prisoners alone. The magnificent behaviour of the infantry units is deserving of the highest commendation, and in deploring the loss of those gallant comrades who have given their lives for their King and Country, Sir Henry Rawlinson hopes that all Officers and men fully realize that what they have accomplished, in breaking through the German line, is an achievement of which they should all feel justly proud."

THE LATE COLONEL LAURIE.

To the Editor of the "Irish Times."

Sir,

I was moved even to tears, which I trust were not unmanly, at your touching reference to the glorious death, last Sunday, of my dear, lamented friend, Colonel Laurie, who would, I had hoped, in the course of nature, have survived me for many a year. It may, perhaps, be of interest to your readers to know that this gallant soldier, who—I can speak with some knowledge—proved himself excellent in every relation of life, and who, *felix opportunitate mortis*, died for us and for our liberties at the head of a renowned Irish regiment—the Royal Irish Rifles—had, though not himself an Irishman, connections and associations with this country of which he was justly proud. His wife is a great granddaughter of the Right Hon. John Foster (Lord Oriel), the last Speaker of the Irish House of Commons. He himself was the great-grandson of an illustrious Irishman, Dr. Inglis, the Bishop of Nova Scotia, who was the first Anglican Colonial Bishop ever consecrated—a Trinity College, Dublin, man, and the son of a rector of Ardara, in Donegal. Dr. Inglis emigrated to America, and was, on the eve of the War of the American Independence, Rector of Holy Trinity Church, New York, then (and I believe now) the principal Anglican Episcopal Church in that city. Dr. Inglis was a pronounced loyalist. He was warned not to read the State prayers for the King and the Parliament. He disregarded the warning. His reading of those prayers was interrupted by forced coughs and sneezings and other manifestations of disfavour. He was then the recipient of many threatening letters. On the next Sunday his voice, when reading the obnoxious prayers, was drowned by a clattering of arms. On the Sunday following guns were actually levelled at him as he read the prayers quite undismayed, having, like his great-grandson, the heart and courage of a hero. Yielding to the entreaties of friends, he left New York for Canada, and on his return, more than twenty years afterwards, to New York, when Bishop of Nova Scotia, he disinterred a magnificent silver coffee pot which he had buried on the eve of his hurried departure, and found in the place he had left it. That coffee pot is a precious heirloom in Colonel Laurie's family. There is a brass tablet to the memory of Dr. Inglis in St. Patrick's Cathedral, erected there by the enthusiasm of Chancellor H.V. White, Rector of St. Bartholomew's, whose own ministry was for some years in the Colonies.

Colonel Laurie's father, General J.W. Laurie, C.B.[13], served with great distinction in the Crimea, where he was twice wounded; in the Indian Mutiny, and in the Transvaal. He was Honorary Colonel of the Royal Munster Fusiliers, and, having sat for some years in the Canadian House of Commons, was from 1895 till 1906 Unionist Member in the Imperial Parliament for the Pembroke Burghs, and a prime favourite with all sorts and conditions of men in the House of Commons. Colonel Laurie's elder brother, Captain Haliburton Laurie, who was one of the most deservedly loved men of his generation, fell in the Boer War in 1901. If he had not been a great soldier, Colonel Laurie would have been a great historian. His knowledge of history, more especially of military history, was profound, and his memory was singularly retentive. He had, moreover, a very sound judgment in the marshalling of facts. He had written with a pen of light the history of his regiment, which he loved, and which loved him, and on which in life and in death he had shed additional lustre.

Yours, etc.,
J.G. Swift MacNeill.

DUBLIN, *March 20th, 1915.*

(*From the "Irish Telegraph," March 20th, 1915.*)

R.I. RIFLES ENGAGED.

Lieut.-Colonel Laurie Killed.
Other Regimental Losses.

Information reached Belfast yesterday that Lieutenant-Colonel George Brenton Laurie, commanding the 1st Battalion Royal Irish Rifles, was killed in action, near Neuve Chapelle, last Sunday. The deceased officer was exceedingly well known in Belfast, where he commanded the Rifles Depot for three years, and the news of his demise has been received with sorrow at Victoria Barracks. He was closely connected by marriage with the North of Ireland.

Colonel Laurie's Military Career.

Lieutenant-Colonel George Brenton Laurie, Commanding Officer of the 1st Battalion Royal Irish Rifles, who has died a soldier's death at the head of the gallant 83rd, will long be remembered by the old corps, in which he spent thirty years. He was the author of the splendid "History of the Royal Irish Rifles" which was issued last year, and dedicated by him to the regiment on the 125th anniversary of the raising of the 83rd and 86th Foot, now the 1st and 2nd Battalions of the Rifles. He considered the writing of that history, which runs into 540 pages, a fitting close to his career in the regiment, but he remained on in the Service, and the unexpected European War has made it otherwise, and now he has ended his career on the field of battle. The closing words of his preface were:—

"May the officers and men of the Royal Irish Rifles win yet more laurels for their regiment by their staunchness whenever their Sovereign calls for their services in war!"

When Colonel Laurie penned those words last spring, he little dreamt that within a few short months the officers and men of both the 83rd and 86th would be shedding their life's blood freely in France, and now he himself has made the supreme sacrifice, and with Captains Master, Reynolds, Davis, Kennedy, Stevens, Allgood, Whelan, Miles, Biscoe, Lieutenants Rea, Whitfield, Burges, and Tyndall, Second-Lieutenants Magenis, Davy, Gilmore, Swaine, and Eldred—many of them his old comrades—sleeps his last long sleep in a foreign grave.

The son of a soldier (the late General Laurie), Colonel Laurie received his first commission in the Rifles in September, 1885, and joined the 2nd

Battalion, then quartered at Halifax, the last station occupied by British infantry in Canada, and it is interesting to recall that he was the last officer to join the battalion with the rank of Lieutenant, as an Army Order issued some time later directed subalterns to begin service as Second-Lieutenants. Halifax, Colonel Laurie tells us in his history of the regiment, was a delightful station, and all were sorry to leave it, the men especially so, and over 300 of them gave in their names as married without leave. Lieutenant Laurie moved with the battalion to Gibraltar in November, 1886, and to Egypt in January, 1888. In 1889 Lieutenant Laurie went up the Nile with the battalion, which was detained at Assouan so long that it missed the fight at Toski. He afterwards served at Malta and in various home stations, and did not again see active service until 1901, when he was sent from England as a special service officer for mounted infantry work, and took command of No. 2 Mounted Infantry Company of the 2nd Battalion of the Rifles.

In the action at Hartbeestefontein he had a narrow escape, riding some 300 yards in front of his company in a charge, with one corporal. They were surprised from a house at 25 yards range, and the corporal saved his life by shooting a man in the act of aiming at his officer.

He distinguished himself in the action at Klerksdorp and in the pursuit of Niewhoudt's commando, and on February 26th, 1902, was ordered to Pretoria to take command of the 28th Battalion Mounted Infantry, handing over his company to Lieutenant Low, who was killed a fortnight later. Captain Laurie was highly commended by Colonel Rochfort for his services with the Rifles Mounted Infantry in these words:—

"During the whole of my time in South Africa I did not command better or more mobile troops than the two mounted infantry companies of the Royal Irish Rifles under Captain Laurie and Captain Baker."

For his services in the war Captain Laurie was mentioned in despatches, and received the Queen's medal with clasps. A step in rank came in 1904, and in 1911 Major Laurie had the honour of commanding the detachment of the 2nd Royal Irish Rifles which was sent from Dover to London to attend the Coronation of King George. On October 28th, 1912, Major Laurie was promoted to the command of the 1st Battalion, then at Kamptee, Lieutenant-Colonel O'Leary's term having expired. He brought the regiment from India to Aden, and last October it was moved to England prior to going to France in the following month.

("Belfast Newsletter," March 20th, 1915.)

FROM NEUVE CHAPELLE.

Belfast Regiment's Part.
Heroism of Colonel Laurie.

Interesting particulars of the part played by the 1st Battalion Royal Irish Rifles in the attack on Neuve Chapelle are given by Sergeant-Major Miller, who is now in the Mater Misericordiæ Hospital, Dublin, with a severe wound in the eye received on that occasion. The Rifles formed part of the Fourth Army Corps, which, with the Indian Corps, as reported by Field-Marshal French, carried out the assault on the German lines. Prior to the action General Sir Henry Rawlinson inspired his troops with an address, in which he said:—

"The attack which we are about to undertake is of the first importance to the Allied cause. The army and the nation are watching the result, and Sir John French is confident that every individual in the Fourth Army Corps will do his duty and inflict a crushing defeat on the German Seventh Corps, which is arrayed against us."

This, says the sergeant-major, was the only intimation of the enemy's strength. Had it been otherwise, the result would have been the same. On the first day of the attack their Commanding Officer, Colonel Laurie, seemed to have a charmed life. He deliberately walked up and down, giving orders and cheering the men on amid a flood of fire. He seemed unconscious of the fact that a great bombardment was taking place. It was a wonderful sight to see him there, his big military figure standing out boldly in presence of his soldiers. Colonel Laurie and his adjutant were killed the next day, in spite of the charm which seemed to surround his life on the previous day. The sergeant-major is unable to state how many men the Rifles lost. He is getting on favourably, and comrades from the 3rd Battalion at Wellington Barracks are permitted to visit him.

Sergeant Murphy, of the 3rd Battalion of the Rifles, has received a letter from his brother (who was wounded with the Rifles at Neuve Chapelle, and is now in hospital at Brighton), in which he says:—"I think I am a lucky man to get away at all. Our Commanding Officer, Colonel Laurie, was killed, and all our officers have been nearly washed out. There was an awful bombardment between the two armies, and it was only a very odd man that got away without being wounded. The Germans lost heavily; so did we. I was in a ward with the Germans, and they told me they were glad they got wounded, for they would have to be killed anyway."

Rifleman Sharkey, who was wounded, and is in hospital at Netley, writes:—"We got a bad cutting-up, and lost our beloved Colonel and adjutant and the two officers of our company."

("Morning Post," September 20th, 1916.)

THE ROYAL IRISH RIFLES.

ULSTER GALLANTRY.

(From a Military Correspondent.)

"Well done; very well done indeed." Such was the remark of a General standing at a Ginchy débris heap as the Irish battalions moved past him on the way to a rest point in the captured line. The numbering of the platoons did not reach the morning's total, but the men had conquered, and they bore aloft the trophies of the battle, helmets and such like, which they waved at the General. All had contributed to the joy of Ireland from Cork to Derry, Ulsterman and Nationalist, and the Royal Irish Rifles had made Belfast glad.

Colonel Fitch raised the regiment in Dublin six score years ago, and the Army of that time called them "Fitch's Grenadiers," because the men were small of stature. When they fought they were as giants, and later on the good physique of the men and their hardy endurance earned them the name of the "Irish Giants." One branch of the regiment was raised in County Down, and to-day the name is perpetuated in the 4th and 5th Battalions, which are known as the Royal Down Militia, despite official changes of designation; and as a further link with the past the depot is in Belfast and the Record Office in Dublin.

When mobilization was ordered, one battalion of the Royal Irish Rifles was scorching under the sun at Aden, and the other was at Tidworth, on Salisbury Plain. The former were to take over the barracks of the latter, which unit was to commence at Malta, in the Winter of 1914, and a tour of service abroad. The latter, however, went out with their Tidworth comrades. It would be covering very old ground to repeat what magnificent work was done in the Great Retreat, when the Royal Irish Rifles showed themselves possessed of the grit which had characterised them at Stormberg, where the writer witnessed them scaling the face of a cliff of rock to get at the Boers, who had ambushed Gatacre's force—an unforgettable and heroic sight. In the retreat towards Paris and the advance to the Aisne Lieutenant-Colonel W.D. Bird, Major C.R. Spedding, and a dozen others were mentioned by Lord French, and a D.S.O., a Military Cross, several D.C.M.'s, a Médaille Militaire, and a special promotion resulted, this being the beginning of many subsequent rewards.

In the Ypres—Armentières phase of the campaign, when the British Army skilfully withdrew to the north of the line, the 7th Brigade repulsed heavy assaults, and both battalions of the Royal Irish Rifles added to their lists of distinguished names. The victory at Neuve Chapelle further increased the record of the regiment, whose men charged the enemy in splendid fashion. Lieutenant-Colonel Laurie was killed, and his adjutant, Captain Wright, fell by his side, while Major Alston was also killed. All three were mentioned in despatches, as well as a score of others. At Hooge the Royal Irish Rifles tried to force their way into the enemy's lines through uncut entanglement in the face of machine-gun fire, and their conduct all through the Loos operations was evidence of the high character of the regiment.

In the operations under Sir Douglas Haig in the early part of 1916 trench warfare, with its brilliant raids, two battalions were named for distinguished conduct, and the numbers as well as the names of the battalions were published in the list issued to the Press.

When the great advance began on July 1st, the Ulster Division attacked the strongest position in the line, and suffered heavily. An officer, describing this glorious attack, wrote:—"I am not an Ulsterman, but as I followed the amazing attack of the Ulster Division on July 1st, I felt that I would rather be an Ulsterman than anything else in the world." With shouts of "Remember the Boyne" and "No surrender, boys," they threw themselves at the Germans, and before they could be restrained had penetrated to the enemy's fifth line. The Royal Irish Rifles went through hell that day, and sought out the machine gunners at the bayonet's point. There has been nothing finer in the war than this charge.

What the regiment did at Guillemont and Ginchy is the talk of the moment, for, with the other Irish battalions, they accounted for all who came in their front—Guards, Line, and guns. Perhaps the two latest awards are among the best. The Victoria Cross was won by Privates Robert Quigg and William McFadzean. The former went out seven times in the heaviest fire for wounded men. The latter gave his life for his comrades by throwing himself on the top of two bombs and taking the whole force of the two explosions. He was blown to pieces. There are many other battle phases and incidents worthy of record, but that which has been written is enough to show what the old 83rd and 86th Foot, the men of County Down, Belfast, Antrim, the Young Citizens, and the others have done, and are doing, in this tremendous combat.

SPECIAL ORDER OF THE DAY BY HIS MAJESTY THE KING.[14]

Officers, Non-Commissioned Officers and Men—

I am very glad to have been able to see my Army in the Field.

I much wished to do so in order to gain a slight experience of the life you are leading.

I wish I could have spoken to you all, to express my admiration of the splendid manner in which you have fought and are still fighting against a powerful and relentless enemy.

By your discipline, pluck and endurance, inspired by the indomitable regimental spirit, you have not only upheld the tradition of the British Army, but added fresh lustre to its history.

I was particularly impressed by your soldierly, healthy, cheerful appearance.

I cannot share in your trials, dangers and successes; but I can assure you of the proud confidence and gratitude of myself and of your fellow countrymen.

We follow you in our daily thoughts on your certain road to victory.

GEORGE, R.I.
December 5th, 1914.

GENERAL HEADQUARTERS.

R.I.R.'s AT NEUVE CHAPELLE.

[A Poem written by Rifleman J. Dickson.]

DEAR FRANC,

Just a few lines of verse about the Royal Irish Rifles at Neuve Chapelle.—Yours truly,

No. 9180 Rifleman J. Dickson,
"A" Coy., 3rd Battalion Royal Irish Rifles, Dublin.

Come, please just pay attention, and a story I will tell Of how the gallant R.I.R.'s were the first in Neuve Chapelle;Colonel Laurie gave the order for the regiment to advance,And when they met the Germans our boys did make them dance.

With bayonets fixed we rushed them, though outnumbered five to one;Each one did prove a hero, and many a gallant deed was done;Our noble Colonel, he was killed, our Major fell as well,And a score of our brave officers lost their lives at Neuve Chapelle.

Our men were lost in hundreds, no regiment could do more,And when the fight was over our officers numbered four;Yet manfully they struggled amidst that living hell,And out of all the British Army were the first in Neuve Chapelle.

Then here's to the gallant R.I.R., those riflemen so brave,Who nobly did their duty and found a soldier's grave;So may their glory ever shine, for they have proved their worth,And laurels brought to Ireland for the honour of the North.

"THE MAN OF SORROWS."

God hath sent thee many trials,But strength is as thy day;Do not despair or say, my child,"I have no heart to pray."For God's ways are not your ways,And tho' thou art bereftOf all that's most endearing,There is one comfort left.

When a dear one has departedTo enter into rest,And you feel so broken-heartedThat you cannot say "'Tis best";There is One Who will always help youAnd bring you great relief:For He was a Man of SorrowsAnd acquainted sore with grief.

When your dearest idol's takenAnd you are dumb with pain;When your faith in man is shakenAnd everything seems vain,There is One you can rely on,Tho' of sinners you are chief:For He was a Man of SorrowsAnd acquainted sore with grief.

Oh! weary, wandering, wilful child,Think of that dying thief,Who sought his Saviour, e'en tho' late,In the bitterness of grief;And say no more you are alone,Bereft of every friend:The Man of Sorrows is your stayAnd comfort to the end.

—Dorcas Skeffington.

FOOTNOTES:

[1] Major Herbert Stepney, Irish Guards, was killed while commanding the Battalion in the first Battle of Ypres.

[2] Major Osbert Clinton-Baker, of Bayfordbury, Hertfordshire, Second-in-Command 1st Battalion Royal Irish Rifles, gazetted Colonel of the Regiment in May, about two months after Colonel Laurie fell. He was mortally wounded and missing at Fromelles on May 9th, 1915.

[3] Capt. Haliburton Laurie fell in the South African War at Philippolis, on a kopje, while rescuing a wounded patrol.

[4] Afterwards Brigadier-General Napier. Previous to the war he commanded the 2nd Bn. Royal Irish Rifles in Aldershot and Dover. He was killed while landing troops in Gallipoli during the summer of 1915.

[5] Sir Nevil Macready, at this time Adjutant-General of our Forces.

[6] The number of killed amounted to 44 and 88 wounded.

[7] Colonel Horsborgh was taken ill suddenly on the transport returning from Aden, and he was buried at sea by Colonel Laurie.

[8] See page 119.

[9] General Laurie and his brother. Colonel Dyson-Laurie, went to the Crimean War when quite young boys, aged respectively 18 and 15. Appended is an article written by the former, and is of interest in drawing a contrast between the conditions of war in 1854 and those of the late war.

[10] Brigadier-Gen. Lowry Cole fell in action at the Battle of Fromelles, May 9th, 1915.

[11] General Bird commanded the 2nd Bn. Royal Irish Rifles, and was through the severe fighting of the Battle of the Aisne and the Retreat from Mons, where he was terribly wounded and lost his leg.

[12] Lieut. W.F.E. Denison (Sherwood Foresters) served in the Great War, and fell mortally wounded in the last German advance near Cambrai on March 24th, 1918.

[13] Civil and Military.

[14] See page 29.

CPSIA information can be obtained
at www.ICGtesting.com
Printed in the USA
LVHW030141271222
735871LV00001B/232